THE JOY OF BELIEVING

THE JOY OF BELIEVING

by
MADELEINE DELBRÊL

Introduction by Archbishop José H. Gomez
Preface by Jean Guéguen
Foreword by Guy Lafon

Translated by James Henri McMurtrie

SOPHIA INSTITUTE PRESS
Manchester, New Hampshire

Sophia Institute Press

Box 5284, Manchester, NH 03108

1-800-888-9344

www.SophiaInstitute.com

Sophia Institute Press is a registered trademark of Sophia Institute.

paperback ISBN 978-1-64413-904-2

ebook ISBN 978-1-64413-905-9

Library of Congress Control Number: 2023943679

Contents

PART II
A Life of Contradiction

PART III
Our Daily Bread

PART IV
Apostolic Life

PART V
Prayer

PART VI
Alcide, or the Perfect Little Monk: A Simple
Guide for Simple Christians

Introduction

HOLINESS IS THE SECRET key that unlocks the inner meaning of history. Through the lives of the saints, God reveals His intentions in history and shows us how we should walk in the footsteps of Jesus Christ. And in every time and place, the saints are the true agents of change and renewal, not only in the Church but also in the wider world.

The twentieth was one of history's most violent and war-torn centuries, marked by atheistic, anti-human revolutions and ideologies that continue today. But in that century, God raised up some of the Church's greatest saints and blesseds, a beautiful array of holy and heroic men and women, fascinating characters such as Mother Teresa, John Paul II, Padre Pio, Charles de Foucauld, Joesemaría Escrivá, Maximilian Kolbe, Teresa Benedicta of the Cross (Edith Stein), Miguel Pro, Gianna Molla, José Sánchez del Río, Irmã Dulce Pontes, and Chiara Badano.

These saints were witnesses to hope in dark times, shining the light of Christ and His truth and showing us the path to holiness and love in times marked by evil and great suffering.

There were other heroic and holy figures, too, not canonized but no less important and inspiring. Among my favorites are the Servants of God Dorothy Day and Sr. Thea Bowman and Ven. Madeleine Delbrêl. Each of these women followed Christ with a zeal to save souls and a deep passion for the poor and the marginalized; they hungered for holiness and drank deeply from the Church's rich traditions of prayer and spiritual life.

Ven. Madeleine Delbrêl was born in southwest France in 1904. She was a creative, passionate soul; she played the piano and wrote poetry, and she loved to dance.

Early on, she lost her faith in God. "By the time I was fifteen," she would later write, "I was a strict atheist, and the world grew for me more absurd by the day." At seventeen, she wrote a manifesto that she titled "God Is Dead ... Long Live Death."

Talking to students many years later, in 1960, she recalled: "At the time, I would have given the whole world to know why I was in it."

That was not the end of her story; God was not done with her. Some Christians befriended her and encouraged her to pray and read the Gospels. She opened the door of her heart and found that Jesus Christ had been standing there knocking all along (Rev. 3:20).

"By reading and reflecting I found God," she would later say. "But by praying I believed that God found me and that He is a living reality, and that we can love Him in the same way that we can love a person."

Seeking guidance and spiritual direction, she went to a priest, Fr. Jacques Lorenzo, then a pastor in Paris. For more than a year in spiritual direction, he opened the Scriptures to her. It changed her life: "He made the Gospel explode for me ... not only [as] the book of the living Lord, but also the Lord's book to live by."

With Fr. Lorenzo's encouragement, she trained as a nurse and a social worker. At age twenty-nine in 1933, along with three other laywomen, Madeleine founded a contemplative community in Ivry, a communist-run suburb of Paris. The women took vows of celibacy and lived a life of manual labor and prayer among the poor, offering hospitality and works of mercy. Ven. Madeleine lived in Ivry for more than thirty years, until her death in 1964. She said she went there because, "in Ivry, men were unbelieving and poor."

For her, this Marxist city became a modern mission territory, and she carried out her mission not by preaching but by her presence, by her love and friendship. Sharing in the ordinary lives of her neighbors, living her faith with joy and fraternity and with deep concern for those around her, she allowed the joy and love of God to break into a darkened world.

Sophia Institute Press is to be applauded for bringing out this book, which is one of the few collections of her writings in English and has long been out of print. It is time for a new generation to meet Madeleine Delbrêl, who was declared Venerable by Pope Francis in 2018.

"We, the ordinary people of the street," Ven. Madeleine used to say, "believe with all our might that this street, this world, where God has placed us, is our place of holiness."

Madeleine, like so many saints from the last century, shows us that holiness is not only something for those set apart from the world in monasteries or convents. She reminds us that saints are people we meet every day on the streets, people whom God places in the crowds, to work ordinary jobs and meet the everyday challenges of living their Christian faith in an often hostile secular world.

In Ven. Madeleine we see an anticipation of the spirituality of the Second Vatican Council (1962–1965). The work of Church councils has been compared to planting seed. It takes time, sometimes centuries, for their fruits to develop fully.

For me, Vatican II's most beautiful "seed" is its teaching on "the universal call to holiness." In the Council's document on the Church, *Lumen Gentium* (Light of the Nations), we read:

> In the Church, everyone ... is called to holiness.... The Lord Jesus, the divine Teacher and Model of all perfection, preached holiness of life to each and everyone of His

> disciples of every condition.... They must follow in His footsteps and conform themselves to His image seeking the will of the Father in all things. They must devote themselves with all their being to the glory of God and the service of their neighbor. (39–40)

The Council rediscovered the key to Jesus' teaching in the Sermon on the Mount: "You, therefore, must be perfect, as your heavenly Father is perfect" (Matt. 5:48). To be perfect means to be holy, as God is holy. And holiness means the perfection of love.

The truth that Jesus preached and the Council rediscovered is that each of us is created to be a saint. All of us in the Church are called to holiness, each in our own way. Holiness is our vocation and duty, yours and mine. It is the purpose of our lives. As St. Paul taught: "This the will of God, your sanctification" (1 Thess. 4:3).

In the figure of Madeleine Delbrêl, we understand that holiness is also apostolic. To be a disciple of Jesus Christ is to be a missionary; it means sharing in His mission of salvation.

Madeleine believed that the Church's mission depends on each one of us, no matter who we are or what our state in life. Either evangelize or stop calling yourself a Christian: that is the blunt message of one of her retreat conferences, "Christian Mission or Abdication," included in this book.

"Mission means doing the very work of Christ wherever we happen to be," Madeleine said. "We will not be the Church, and salvation will not reach the ends of the earth, unless we help save the people in the very situations in which we live."

Read these pages carefully, with prayer. Madeleine is a quiet, powerful writer, deceptively simple, but her writing contains multitudes. It pays to read her slowly, turning her words over in your mind, pondering them. These words were written in prayer and contemplation, and they should be read that way too.

The Joy of Believing is a window into the soul of a twentieth-century apostle who lived and worked in the heart of an unbelieving world. Here you will find expressions of the faith that sustained her: prayer, meditations, poems, essays, retreat notes, talks she gave to her community. In these pages, you find her intimate reflections on the Beatitudes, the Eucharist, prayer, and the demands of following Jesus in a world where He has been forgotten.

Ven. Madeleine Delbrêl was a mystic as well as a missionary. She had a profound sense that in the Gospels we truly encounter the Word made flesh:

> The words of the Gospel are miraculous. If they don't transform us, it's because we don't ask them to. But the staggering virtue that healed, purified, and revived people remains in each of Jesus' phrases and examples....
>
> When we hold our Gospel in our hands, we should think that the Word lives in it. He wants to become flesh in us and take hold of us. This is so that with His heart, grafted onto our hearts, and His Spirit, connected to our spirits, we'll restart His life in another place, time, and human society.
>
> Examining the Gospel in this way entails surrendering our lives in order to receive a destiny that's completely formed after Christ's likeness.

In her reading of the Gospel and her reception of the Eucharist, Madeleine was being transformed by Jesus, day by day, into His own likeness. In her mystical sensibility she reminds me of St. Paul, who spoke of being changed into the Lord's likeness, from glory to glory. Paul also said: "It is no longer I who live, but Christ who lives in me" (Gal. 2:20; see 2 Cor. 3:18).

Madeleine's mysticism did not take her out of the world. Instead, it plunged her deeper into the heart of the world, with all its pain, poverty, and injustice. She wanted to live and to love as Jesus did, and she wanted to do that in our age and in our society. She wanted to meet Jesus and follow Him in the concrete conditions of everyday life:

> Another day is starting.
> Jesus wants to live it in me. He hasn't shut Himself out. He walked among people. He's with me among the people I encounter today....
> All of them will be people He's come looking for — those He's come to save....
> Jesus is still everywhere. We can't prevent ourselves from being God's representatives at any moment.
> Jesus is present throughout this day, which we share with the people of our time and of all time — both those of my city and the whole world.
> Through the brothers and sisters who are close to us, whom He will make us to serve, love, and save, waves of His love will go out to the end of the world and the end of time.
> Blessed be this new day, which is Christmas for the earth, since Jesus wants to live it in me again.

So, I urge you: take and read. And pray. This is an important, timely, and beautiful book for modern apostles.

I pray that through her words and her spirit, Ven. Madeleine Delbrêl will help all of us in the Church to go deeper in our transformation in the likeness of Jesus Christ. May she help us also to discover, as she did, that our ordinary daily lives are "our place of holiness."

Most Reverend José H. Gomez
Archbishop of Los Angeles
Feast of the Transfiguration of the Lord
August 6, 2023

Note: Biographical details and quotations not found in this volume are from Charles F. Mann, *Madeleine Delbrêl: A Life Beyond Boundaries* (Beijing: New World Press, 1996), and Madeleine Delbrêl, *We, the Ordinary People of the Streets* (Grand Rapids, MI: Eerdmans, 2000 [1966]).

Preface

CARDINAL VEUILLOT HAD FOLLOWED the research of Madeleine Delbrêl and her team since 1954 — first in Rome, and then in Angers and Paris. He intended to introduce the reader to the texts that are collected here.

In May 1967, he expressed the value he placed on this action in these words: "I promise to write a few words about Madeleine. This will hardly go beyond two pages, because I'm overwhelmed by work. I'm going to go on vacation with my breviary, my Gospel, and the future book's manuscript. I'm very keen on it. I'm so grateful to Madeleine!"

The cardinal was prevented from carrying out his intention because of his fatigue, an overloaded schedule, and finally, the sickness that was to take him away.

He confided his regret about not being able to pay his debt of gratitude on his hospital bed and added: "Madeleine's secret of life is a union with Jesus Christ such that it allowed her to be completely bold and free. This is why her love was very real for everyone."

We cannot separate this book from the memory of the archbishop of Paris, who recently passed away.

J. G.
G. L.
1968

"Rome, the Land of My Soul"

Having lived in Rome in 1952, I learned one day, through a letter from one of her friends, that Madeleine Delbrêl intended to bring the missionary anxiety of her time and team to St. Peter's. The letter announcing her arrival described her as "a heart that's expanded to its limits by the Lord's love."

She was entitled to the "fate" of all her friends — a guest house reservation and a trip to the Vatican for a hearing. I didn't see anybody on that day. A few days later, I came across a letter in the mail that Madeleine wished to address to Pius XII, which was forwarded to its recipient:

> For eighteen years, I shared the life of a people who were not only without faith, but without a Christian memory. I was very deeply connected to what the Church in France offers that is both new and long-established. I was persuaded that our faithfulness requires a missionary zeal that's ever more ardent, as well as more strongly rooted in obedience. I wanted to go to Rome in the name of us all, in order to ask Christ's Church for a dual grace.
>
> In order for it to be an act of faith and nothing more, I arrived in Rome in the morning. I went straight to St. Peter's tomb in front of the altar where you celebrate your

Mass. I stayed there the whole day and returned to Paris that night.

I didn't think I had the right to ask Your Holiness for an audience.

Some friends who knew about my trip were kind enough to request it for me.

Because of practical complications, I only found out last night, through a letter to which the ticket for the audience was attached, that You had granted me this audience, and I wasn't there.

I don't know what is greater in me — gratitude or pain. To tell you it's neither one nor the other appears to be impossible for me.

Perhaps it isn't normal to write to the Sovereign Pontiff like this. But when a father has waited for his child, and this child hasn't come, he wouldn't be a child if he didn't write his gratitude and apologies to his father.

Most Holy Father, I ask you to be kind enough to bless me along with all those with which my soul is full by presenting them to you.

Madeleine Delbrêl

Through the same correspondence, I'd know her care in clearly expressing her intentions and those of the group that she was hosting.

We're not specialists in anything. This makes us more flexible to enter a new path. We're in contact, not only with nonbelievers, but also with many Christians variously engaged. That helps us reach the heart of the difficulties on both sides, along with their graces, perils, contrasts, and interdependence.

After a number of events that occurred these last few months, I really wanted to go to Rome. For me, Rome is a kind of sacrament of Christ's Church. It seemed to me that some graces that are requested for the Church are only obtained in Rome. I wanted to take this step in full faith — to spend a day at St. Peter's and pray there thoroughly. I arrived there safely on May 6 at 8:45 a.m., but I didn't think I was expected there. I went directly to St. Peter's. I came out of there two or three times to eat and shop next door. In addition, I stayed where I thought was the best place for my prayer — the pope's altar and St. Peter's tomb. I took the 10:10 p.m. train again.

I didn't know that I'd make the Holy Father wait, which seemed unthinkable to me. I didn't know how to act with him in normal circumstances and knew it even less in this case.

It seems to me that the best thing to do is to *believe*, above all, that he's the *Father*, and act in the simplicity of this faith.[1] (*May 10, 1952.*)

A whole exchange of letters started. I'd learn about Madeleine's Gascon origins and immediately find myself "mobilized on site" to continue this "indispensable intercession in the name of those who are strongly tempted to refuse vital links with Rome." (October 17, 1952.) I only found out a few years later that Madeleine's youth had been marked by a total loss of faith and a long struggle whose outcome had been a sudden conversion.

I'd received requests for services of all varieties from her that left no doubt that she was very close to Ivry's population. Some notes soon arrived — some thoughts that conveyed an uncommon care, realism, and insight about the events of the Church.

[1]   The quotations followed by a parenthesis indicating a date were obtained from the unpublished correspondence of M. Delbrêl.

In 1952, neither "spring" nor "renewal" were part of the vocabulary. The tumult and warnings kept coming.

Far from deploring the difficulties of the "lives of contemporary faith," Madeleine reacted by asserting the strange and unusual character of belonging to God and the urgency of a "prayer to acquire that basic illumination which is always the first act of love." (*December 17, 1952.*)

In January 1953, the letters increased exponentially. The Rosenberg Affair stirred people's passions. Two convicted people awaited the electric chair in the United States. They were accused of having given the Soviet Union information on the nuclear tests conducted at Los Alamos. Lawyers from several countries were disturbed to note procedural defects of the trial, whose shorthand they studied. One of Madeleine's friends, who was a lawyer in Paris, visited Rome as a representative of French legal initiatives. It was an opportunity for Madeleine to touch "the heart of the Church" for a second time.

> Not knowing anything about Roman matters, I was in no position to discuss the "hows" of the process, but it seemed to me that Christ's "may it be done according to your faith" is so completely true when we address the Church that I dreaded any intrusion of human scheming. You have to look at the Church face to face, as a mother does with her children, and stretch out your hands. The straight line that you let H. pursue put him in contact with this Mother Church — with a pope for whom two of his children exist as soon as their names are mentioned to him, outside all human schemes and worldly power. I'm happy for you, for H., and for me.

> Here are two instances where you have, so to speak, given me an X-ray of the Mystical Body. Pray that we'll be alive there and more and more incorporated into it.

She wanted us to know nothing about the way in which she saw Rome, nor what she anticipated there:

You can say that the *Message de Noël* has impressed many French Christians. It seems to me that everyone can think it was written for his country and that every Christian of goodwill leaves it while being comforted and enlightened about his own guilt, encouraged and humbled. I think I'm going to know it by heart soon. What remains is to live it by heart. Thanks again, and how unfortunate that there aren't more words. Tonight, I also think that God's Wisdom isn't our own. I believe it was really ridiculous to have thought of myself as a mail lady. I gave H. the only tangible thing I had in Rome, and that was you. The foundation of God's plan is essentially a network of circumstances, and what lies in the middle is what both makes and unmakes us. This reveals a whole world of certitudes to me. (*January 13, 1953.*)

Rome's heart needs to be enlightened, and Madeleine knows it. She lives in Ivry, where God is absent. It's a city in which she carefully analyzes all the phenomena that touch her up close — the fear of Christians and the vision that nonbelievers have of the Church's visible actions. Once again, she was reserved about saying what was bothering her so much in Rome:

> The French are talkative, and the people from the South of France even more. If you come someday, I'd really like to talk to you about the issue of Marxism! It's so important to be with Christ in their midst. It's really hard to love them, not for what they have, but for what they lack — and at other times not to run away from them by fleeing from evil. They really need us to love them without loving what they love. They really need to have the gospel brought to them, as well as to learn what makes one love, what makes one hate, and what makes one ridicule others. The smallest epiphany can go so far with each of them because of the "political body" that they make up. (*January 15, 1953.*)

A year went by. In February 1954, she insistently came back to what motivated her love for Rome:

> You're well aware that, more and more often, I visit my mainstay.[2] The Body of Christ's work is rough at this time. To go from one to the other — inside Him — is a terrible walk.
>
> For a long time, I'd been struck by the Holy Father's tendency toward solitude. This seemed to be his way of being with everyone. So, I'd very often asked the Virgin Mary to be *gentle* with him — he who can't call any man "Father."
>
> But it seemed that she hardly listened to me. The spirit of confusion blows here in such contradictory and astonishing ways that we have to acknowledge the action of the father of lies. Mary undoubtedly needed the "other father" so that the first battle line could be in her solitude.
>
> There are times when the truth is so hard to recognize that only suffering — like a blind woman — can serve it. This undoubtedly had to be manifested ... It's up to us to follow. (*February 24, 1954.*)

October 1954 ... She came to Rome a second time. "This was the best trip I've ever made," she recalled:

> To be a naturalized Christian, you have to have suffered at least a little bit. (*October 16, 1954.*)

At this time, Msgr. Montini was named archbishop of Milan. Madeleine reacted:

> My point of view is simply limited. What raw material of suffering the Church needs to steer the Kingdom of

---

[2]   A reference to her whirlwind pilgrimage in Rome in 1952.

God! Thanks for standing by me in Rome through prayer. It's really the land my heart longs for ... and all that's not connected to the heart would never have suspected it. (*October 29, 1954.*)

Later:

I was very bored with Rome all this time, and as I have just turned fifty, I'm wondering if this isn't becoming a habit. The "sufferings of the French" invincibly propel my heart. This was a very excessive ambition for someone who hardly leaves her room. (*December 12, 1954.*)

July 1955. Editing notes in preparation for The Marxist City as Mission Territory *is out of the question. They are piling up. Entire chapters are in their second or even third version. This word accompanied the sending of any of them:*

I tried to intensify in myself the reality of the relationships that Christ wants between each of us and the one that the Church is entrusted with — a plunge into the density of the Mystical Body. Rome continues to be the rock. In order for these stones to continue to be the rock, many lives have to be given to them without any strings attached. (*July 23, 1955.*)

Rome was the "rock," but in 1956, Madeleine didn't hide an inner struggle that seemed to be particularly difficult for her:

This summer was a very hard struggle. It wasn't against scruples but against circumstances. They were events that were merely contradictions, with the only tangible part being the poor and vulnerable human being that I am.

I ask you to pray for me because of my Roman story, in which you have been so involved. I'm no longer certain that it's *mine*. For almost two years, everything has been alternately so relentlessly comical and cruel that I no longer recognize my God in it even by trying (?) to love it to death.

I rested a lot in Côme, but I'm going to Rome like an idiot who plays blind man's bluff.

I beg you to ask God — not for the light or anything else — but to be prevented from being out of tune with who He is or what He wants to do. I wanted to let Him be the judge for those He put next to me, because only He knows what is good. (*October 22, 1956.*)

In June 1959, in other circumstances, she mentioned the mystery of Rome that was both a grace and a trial:

Rome's temptation and seduction will remain in me despite everything. I think you recognize that my hobbyhorse is the solitude that God manages so often to give generously to the Christian. It seems to me that it's a kind of sacrifice for the world and one of the deepest cracks that allows the Lord to infiltrate the earth in His Redemption and through us. (*June 12, 1959.*)

An Apostolic Response

IN 1957, AFTER TWENTY-FOUR *years of reflection in Ivry, Madeleine agreed to edit her notes under the title* The Marxist City as Mission Territory. *She consented to it without any modesty or fear.* "Marxism isn't anchored yet in history. It hasn't attained the stability of the bones of my old compatriots in Dordogne — a little jolt — a fleeting jolt — and points of view that I can think are true today can be temporarily or permanently contradicted by the facts." (*June 17, 1957.*)

The Marxist City as Mission Territory *arrived in its own time. The Church questioned itself in the face of unbelief, and Madeleine perceived the Marxists among the nonbelievers that she rubbed shoulders with day after day. What response will the Church give to these very real attitudes — in this confrontation that priests and Christians experience more and more sorrowfully? Madeleine sketched out a response that she did not claim to be the only one. Being realistic and insistent, she advocated an apostolic love. The very terms that were used to express it left no doubt as to its urgency:* "Won't the living God of the gospel burn us unbearably as long as we haven't shouted His name out loud among those who are in despair without knowing it? If they turn around while hearing us call out to God, it would be the beginning of the only good news for them."[3]

By 1933, the date of her settlement in Ivry, Madeleine had gone from the notion of an "extended" mission — implying departures to faraway places, uprootings, foundations, and settlements which were geographically foreign to established Christianity — to what she called "the mission in depth." Faith is sent forth as such and no longer merely kept like a treasure — as such, it only finds itself at home and at its true stature in difficult situations that provoke and harass it. Madeleine wasn't the type to go along with social expectations. She approached each social contact as a new opportunity or beginning. The state of insecurity, injustice, and poverty — even the scorn of all those who surrounded her — was unbearable for her. She'd expose it in pages that were unusually dense in 1950.[4]

Would she, for all that, lose confidence in the Church and refuse to believe it would be capable of this indispensable response?

> I can only say one thing about the pope after reading his speech to prisoners and the sick.[5] The Church is the greatest of God's miracles and has had mercy on her people. The hearts of the little ones are affected. (*January 19, 1959.*)

Between 1954 and 1960, her correspondence entailed a permanent contrast between her research — with the seriousness she put into it — and the detailed and spirited account of a certain number of anecdotes that illustrate this research and grant us a glimpse of the intensity of her concentration.

> I was talking to a railroad worker in Turin and had told him I had a lot of Italian friends in Paris that I really liked.[6] I

---

[3]   From *We, the Ordinary People of the Streets.*
[4]   Ibid.
[5]   John XXIII's speech after his visit to the prison in Rome and then to a hospital during the week of Christmas, 1958.
[6]   We must recall that Madeleine was the daughter of a railroader.

liked many of their songs. Two young people who were also in the compartment suddenly got up to find enough singers in the rest of the freight car, making for fourteen people in our compartment from Turin to Paris. It turned into an uninterrupted festival — so much so that a poor young woman who had strayed into such bad company found herself unwell when we reached Sens. Our choristers then laid her on a bench and, adapting art to weakness, began to sing a lullaby. People gathered together along the trip on the platforms of the railroad stations to find out what was happening in this loud compartment. Well, these were people from Naples. The soloist who was leading the group was twenty-one years old, and had a sort of musical genius about him. Before parting ways, I left my road companions — who were destitute, despite their apprenticeship contract — with my name, address, and telephone number. A few months later, my soloist, P., arrived at my home in the grip of some housing difficulties. After many various repairs, we saw his wife come (I forgot to tell you that he was married and a father). The whole family left again for Italy. The day before my trip to Lyon, a phone call informed us that P. was in France again, and wanted to see us once more with a friend we didn't know. They lacked only a few things. One was missing a residence permit. The other one didn't have a work permit. Neither of them had housing! So, we spent the holidays as a family and quickly got to work as soon as the offices were open. (H., whose specialty it is, will certainly arrive in Paradise with a pile of foreigners' papers.) Then, we had a festival of Italian music, and we ate spaghetti every night — "living," as Robert Lamoureux would say. We hope to reach a good solution for both of them. (*April 1, 1959.*)

A Single Language

Is FAITH THAT'S "GIVEN by God and foreign to the world" *still capable of being perceived by everything that's foreign to the Church? For Madeleine — this active, determined, and sensitive woman who was deeply attentive — faith was the* "temporal commitment of eternal love." *It needs a clear and precise announcement in order for it be perceived as viable and possible.*

It's not obvious that this was easy for her. The friends in Ivry and elsewhere remember the period when she prayed and searched extensively. "We should adapt to each person's age, capacity, and perspective, saying something new to someone new every time. Then it would seem impossible for Christ not to be proclaimed and for the Church, here, to no longer grow."

One of the privileged languages of faith is goodness — real goodness coming from God's heart. It's a clear and direct language, "which doesn't need a translator," "that awakens and questions the heart's dormant forces." *This language impels the Christian to be willing to meet others.* "He becomes everyone's neighbor, with an existence sufficiently open to be known."

The events of her life seemed to embody this language: "Inventive minds and heroic innovations" *found an echo in Madeleine. She didn't stop accepting invitations and expressing herself about her discoveries, and she wasn't satisfied with merely proposing the language of faith as a solution. She began by using it herself. The composition of* The Marxist City *was laborious and long. Its multiple versions were carried from Rome to Milan. This allowed Madeleine to have contacts where she could hold on to this clear language.*

One night, an envelope arrived that was worded this way: Madeleine Delbrêl, IVRY (sic), Francia. Origin: Milan. "Gentillissima Signorina ... I know how lovingly and patiently you prepared The Marxist City as Mission Territory. I'm glad to be tired in such a good way, because you're going to do a lot of good."[7] *The letter was handwritten, written in Italian, and signed by Archbishop G.B. Montini. It prompted the following comment:*

> This letter reminded me once again that I knew a lot of Italian. There are writings that speak an international language, and I think that I would have understood even in Chinese that I received a blessing that fills me with joy and gratitude.[8] (*September 28, 1957.*)

As an advocate of clear and direct language, could Madeleine have accepted not taking great care in everything she wrote? She had a fluid and lively style of writing. But she hadn't written for the sheer pleasure of it in a long time.

> I no longer wish to undertake comprehensive work, but rather to let a file on different aspects of the subject be formed by following life itself, whether to provide specific notes to those in need or to work on it and write it up as required. This seems to me the best way to avoid falling,

---

[7] Madeleine put "good" in quotation marks in a translation of the letter.

[8] Don Macchi, Msgr. Montini's secretary, and later Paul VI's private secretary, was the first to ask for his enrollment in the Association of the Friends of Madeleine Delbrêl.

someday or another, into "literature," which would seem to me the worst of evils. (*March 15, 1956.*)

Her openness, sensitivity, and the tone of truthfulness which she felt she had to give to her love, very often obliged her to take back her papers, tear them up, even mock them, and then completely rewrite them. She feared seeing them circulate without putting the finishing touches on them.

The people in our group agreed with my notes. I wanted to rewrite them. As you have them now, they are not at all right. They are well advanced in their corrections. But I wouldn't have wanted to jeopardize my sleep. That would not have been honest. (*August 24, 1957.*)

Life is a good teacher, and what one can observe in six months without even being aware of it is quite extraordinary. I thought it was stupid not to have written a comprehensive treatment of the issue, and not to propose practical solutions. Certain sections of my work flinched and retreated at the first sign of difficulty, took up too much space, or else were simply weak. All of this led me to work far into the night. Since August I have been increasingly drawn by a selfish desire which is beginning to seem necessary to me: to use a few hours to sleep, and to go on a quarter tour of France for various reasons. (*February 6, 1956.*)

The Church Is Everything

THE LIFE OF FAITH *and clear language of love made Madeleine a woman who was unusually equitable.*

Was she going to embark on an easy criticism of institutions or re-nounce a certain category of Christians? A note had been sent to her one day against some Christians who were said to be reactionary:

> I think the attitudes mentioned have been accurately de-scribed, because I've often met people like this, just as the consequences of such attitudes have been accurately de-scribed. I've also encountered these consequences! But I think there's a great deal of interest in not allowing our-selves to withdraw into an attitude that would only be critical and severe toward these Christian individuals. It seems to me that this sterilizes our efforts upfront and risks making us replace our undeniable failures to love with other failures to love that are no less indisputable. I don't think one can always, or even often, correct such situations without there being some tumult and discon-tent. But I believe that one should not have to reproach oneself for a firmness that is not accompanied by genuine warmth of heart and demanding charity. In the face of

such stumbling blocks, it's easy to be strongly tempted. In such circumstances, an example of the Curé d'Ars comes to mind. When he needed to be severe with a certain great sinner, he supported his severity with painful exclamations, "That's a pity!" and cried about it. We, on the other hand, don't feel like crying, but feel like being caustic sometimes and harsh at other times.

I think it's useful to be vigilant, not only for the truth of things itself, but also to ensure that words of this kind do not hurt those to whom they are communicated, especially when these individuals are situated in a broad perspective of the Church where they must ensure the well-being of very different people. (*February 9, 1959.*)

That same year — 1959 — she wrote in a note:

We should be cautious of a tendency, perhaps acquired in the search for an overly externalized testimony, to "capture" life in snapshots, to turn it into characteristic scenes. Everything that is both Christian and understandable to people translates truthfully in that approach; however, the fact of not revealing the kind of depth that the mystery holds or minimizing the suggestion that can be made of it leads to a truth that is either "diminished" or "tarnished."

Some friendship connections united her to Poland. Rome provided her with opportunities to make several contacts. She went to Africa. In France itself, she worked regularly with various missionary teams or friends who were in Marseilles, Toulouse, and Longwy. Different movements invited her to share her experience. As the Second Vatican Council approached, a bishop from Madagascar asked her for a meticulous study of atheism. This diversity of contacts and inquiries made to her from all sides, combined with her profound sense of complementarity within the Church, led Madeleine to warn us against the complacency that awaits every believer.

Let's guard ourselves from claiming that we're in a place
from which we can judge the entire world.

*Every Christian in the Church truly has a right to his own place. Even if
certain choices or circumstances attract criticism or ridicule, he continues
to be a member of the Body, which is unified. From 1952 to 1958, it wasn't
inappropriate to read what this witness of the Faith wrote:*

> The most unknown among the baptized is our brother in
> an extraordinary life.[9]

*For Madeleine, the Church didn't want us to be anything but "real people
through who they are and what they do," "creatures who are totally
alive," "living fragments who are enormously active in Jesus Christ's
Mystical Body."[10]*

*In order for the Church to be a place for everyone, it's important for
her to readjust her gestures and attitudes. In a note written in 1959, Madeleine indicated how certain unbelieving circles react to certain external
lifestyles of the Church.*

> The presbytery is often an insurmountable barrier. One
> thing would be crucial for unbelievers: the transparency
> of the life of the priest. The presbytery does not manifest
> a mystery, but it establishes a secret that can so easily be
> said to be a bad secret...
>
> The first suspect is the money the priest lives on. The
> quantity of the money is less important than its "quality."
> To be able to say what it is and where it comes from, to
> fight against its anonymous aspect, and to suppress its ori-
> gins (if these would harm justice) are conditions that we
> can't evade.[11]

---

[9] From *We, the Ordinary People of the Streets.*
[10] Ibid.
[11] An unpublished note from 1959.

For the Church to readjust herself, to stand before the world as Jesus Christ himself, she needs a type of priest whose characteristics Madeleine didn't hesitate to outline:

The priest is no longer just a definition. Everything by which this man is known to his friends, colleagues, and neighbors is unknown in the priest. He must come closer, speak, and react to the circumstances of all. Otherwise, he exists as an idea, not as a living being.

We have to say it again — in an unbelieving environment, it is enough for him to live what is human in his life, and without waiting for exceptional events, he will become someone who is a man of God precisely because he is first and foremost a human being. As for the Christian, called to religious apostolate, whose brilliant yet challenging logic does not promise ease, he will find in the formal demands of priestly life an unwavering call to fidelity. The contrast between the personalities who, luckily for us, are mostly as average as we are, and the divine reality they must signify, the duration, throughout the centuries, of such fragility, and the ease with which the Church commits itself to it, not shying away from any public risk, helps us become simple and confident. If, in certain cases, the priest is tempted to take on more and more of the lives of his brothers in order to help them, to help us, the priest can remind himself that he must increasingly become what he is: a simple priest. (*May 14, 1959.*)

Her Sense of Friendship

MADELEINE WAS IN A *community with many companions.*[12] *Moreover, she was constantly in dialogue with priests, religious, and Christians about their preoccupations. Was this about helping a certain "case," or a certain person who was having a hard time? A whole network of friends was immediately alerted. We were used to getting letters in which she shared her personal feelings in a delicate way*:

> These last few months have been filled with work that I don't particularly enjoy.... I feel the need, because I believe it to be essential, to set aside a few weeks to attend to a few "second-order urgencies" of various kinds that concern me: a week or two of prayer and some indispensable meetings with friends to whom I appear to be quite ungrateful and indifferent ... and from whom I'd like some advice. Finally, in all that, to have some long-neglected dental work completed. You can pray that God's will should properly settle

---

[12] As of 1933, two friends came to join her — then, in thirty years, about fifteen of them. Madeleine guided and hosted the group, which broke up into several "settlements" — Longwy, Abidjan, Tizi-Ouzou — without being divided.

into this plot of land that is my life. I don't know how to interpret it anymore. (*September 27, 1956.*)

The tone of her gratitude doesn't leave any doubt about her sense of friendship:

> I want to thank you for what you've done for me and what I've found myself entrusted with since I've known you. What I am entrusted with — after God, that is — is also because of you. But, unless I am blind, I must acknowledge that this responsibility has coincided, with astonishing precision, with an almost uninterrupted series of events, most of which seemed burdensome to me precisely because they were truly unusual. While, in all areas, the people who should have normally helped or supported me were either on temporary or inexplicable vacations, four individuals whom I did not know before these recent years have helped me without reason. You are among them, and I can tell you that you four, in different areas, have given me incomparably more than you can imagine. (*June 19, 1957.*)

Another Language Is Suffering

SUFFERING DIDN'T FAIL HER. *The abandonment of some friends over a misunderstanding added to a spiritual trial over multiple* "collective and individual betrayals" *resulting, she suggested, from* "an extremely diminished faith in the lives of Christians." (*March 12, 1956.*)

This suffering of the Church, which she deeply understood, would be periodically poured out in Rome "at the Pietà" *of the Basilica of Saint Peter:*

> I hope that Rome nourishes you like a wise and strong mother. Speaking of Mother, would you please greet the Pietà for me? You should remind some French people in Rome to adorn it with flowers. (*January 26, 1959.*)

Would you like a glimpse of her reactions to physical suffering?

> In life, there are those who endure honorable sufferings and those who face humiliating troubles. The Lord put me in the former category. I'm leaving tonight in a very bad mood for one month, to take care of the noble illness known as "fatigue." (*April 9, 1954.*)

Here's the cell, the vigil, and, moreover, the disgust for earthly nourishment. (*Easter Tuesday, 1957.*)

A pitiful condition. I can't do anything. I think I must resign myself to what the Lord is making me recognize — my incapacity — and for tomorrow, no communication. It wouldn't be good to cling to my projects, but rather to see what God wants or doesn't want from my capacities or inabilities. (*May 25, 1957.*)

My health remains unstable, yet it is improving steadily in the most paradoxical circumstances of recovery. Rediscovering, despite an abnormal workload, one by one, the engagements of a normal life is, I fear, a terrestrial but exquisite delight. (*January 26, 1958.*)

These quick overviews and partial incursions into Madeleine Delbrêl's correspondence seek to acknowledge their limitations and — how should I put it? — that appearance of a lack of seriousness that made Madeleine so endearing and, at the same time, so profound.

The format of this presentation has limited these lines to serve as a mere introduction. If these numerous and dense quotations have allowed the reader to enter more deeply into the world of this strongly committed laywoman, then our goal has been achieved! She was both contemplative and communicative with her surroundings, her city, and her neighborhood, as well as realistic in a time and an environment that was challenging for faith.

We will be grateful to Madeleine Delbrêl for instilling a strong hope in our time and dictating to us the way to live it. Fr. Guy Lafon tells us why and how the text is arranged.[13]

JEAN GUÉGUEN

---

[13] The director of the Saint-Sulpice Seminary and a chaplain of the Parisian students of the École Normale.

Foreword

AFTER *THE MARXIST CITY as Mission Territory* and after *We, the Ordinary People of the Streets*, a new book that gathers together Madeleine Delbrêl's writings takes us back to the daily foundations of her life and work. What do we find there?

First of all, a very simple conviction. It's so simple that we don't understand why it should be astonishing: Madeleine thought of the Gospel as a contemporary book — even today, it presents us with possibilities for our own lives. Consequently, there's nothing better to do than familiarize ourselves with it continuously as a guide and a source of strength. "When we hold our Gospel in our hands, we should think that the Word lives in it. He wants to become flesh in us and take hold of us so that with His heart, grafted onto ours, and His spirit connected to our spirit, we start His life over again in another place, time, and human society."[14]

Others besides Madeleine had certainly said that before her. Others besides her had also experienced it. But she had a tone that was hers alone to talk about it and experience it. She, perhaps better than

[14] Page 32.

anyone in our time, perceived and expressed how much of a loss of self faith demands of us. For the Gospel, which is discovered and practiced today and always renews itself, completely "dives into a plan that remains obscure for us."[15] Thus, each person must agree to become unusual to believers and nonbelievers alike" — that is to say, to oneself as well.[16] This is to be done not to taste what is poignant or because of a need to be uncomfortable, but because Jesus always goes about it in this way when He shows His face through a human being."[17]

Madeleine reminds us of the simple joy of believing — of the joy that a ponderous and stiff faith forgets. It often, alas, makes this oblivion a virtue. In the same way, we must relearn that we're immediately called to this because we still need to marvel that God honors us by asking us for something. "We are all predestined to be ecstatic, to get out of our poor connections, and to arise in our plan — one hour after another. We are never lamentable social outcasts."[18] As if to convince us that this joy, which is indeed ours, nevertheless, dwells in us as a gift of our God, Madeleine compares it somewhere to Jesus being born in us again: "Jesus hasn't stopped being the Son in everything. He wants to stay connected to the Father in me — gently connected every second like a cork on the water — gentle like a lamb before every one of its Father's wishes."[19]

An apostolic inquiry will spring up from such an evangelical faith. It's experienced in a serious and joyful tone — as an urgency within our believing being: "Will God continue to be "dead for all those who are beside us — who know that we have given Him our lives, and that we say it and don't regret it. Won't this death be doubted?"[20]

[15] Page 65.
[16] Page 121.
[17] Page 121.
[18] Page 128.
[19] Page 133.
[20] Page 158.

Thus, when the believer encounters the militant ignorance or the refusal of God in the brotherly shoulder to shoulder experiences of daily life, these become bearers of a renewed call for him. He hears something like an exterior echo in them. It reverberates in his brothers' and sisters' spiritual misery and in his vocation to adore God, who is the joy of his life. Atheism seems to be just as unbearable to him, perhaps even more so. But, in a way, it no longer disorients or scares him. "This solemn negation of God irresistibly impels us to remain where it's said that God is dead — to let the name of Jesus Christ, the Lord as well as the living Savior, quickly be inscribed in us. But this name of Jesus Christ, which has been inscribed in us and written on us, must one day publicly become our name either willingly or by force."[21]

This is how Madeleine opened the path of a redeeming life of faith. Who would be surprised that this path would go through prayer and brotherly love that are actually practiced? Madeleine didn't claim to be a spiritual innovator. Her originality, if we must find it here, is to have gently insisted that the children of God were now, as always, called to save the world at their own risk — with and by the strength of the Only Son: "The hope of the apostles of all times is a gigantic beggar whose feet are on a lost world. Its arms are carrying the most darkened people. It's extremely poor with them ... but smiling at a Redemption from Heaven that it waits for as we wait for the day."[22]

Must we be surprised that such intuitions have sometimes been humorous in order to express themselves? It was a modest and happy way — not to conceal oneself — but to step aside. When we're aware, as Madeleine was, of the tragic misfortunate of unbelief, the spirit of seriousness threatens us. Her friends really knew she didn't yield to

[21] Page 161.
[22] Page 151.

this temptation. The character of Alcide, which she had created, testifies to the clearness that she knew how to apply to her thoughts and struggles without being sad about it. Laughter was the other face of Madeleine's joy: "And in this adventure of Mercy, we're asked to give what we can until we're worn out. We're asked to laugh when this gift is missing, sordid, or impure. But we're also asked to marvel with tears of gratitude and joy before this inexhaustible treasure that the Lord pours into us. Our unmistakable peace will move into this intersection of laughter and joy."[23]

[23]   Page 70.

THE JOY OF BELIEVING

PART I

The Gospel is the Book of our Life

"The one who doesn't take the slim book of the Gospel in his hands with the resolution of a person who has only one hope can neither decipher nor receive the message."

We, the Ordinary People of the Streets.

The Lord's Book[1]

THE GOSPEL IS THE book of the Lord's life. It's for our life as well.

It's not made to be understood, but to be approached like something that's on the brink of mystery.

It's not just to be read, but to be received by us.

Each of its words is spirit and life. They are agile and free and await only the eagerness of our souls to become part of us. They are alive like the initial yeast that attacks our dough and makes it ferment with a new way of life.

The words of human books are understood and evaluated.

The words of the Gospel are experienced and endured.

We absorb the words of books. The words of the Gospel shape, modify, and integrate *us* into *them*, so to speak.

The words of the Gospel are miraculous. If they don't transform us, it's because we don't ask them to. But the staggering virtue that healed, purified, and revived people remains in each of Jesus' phrases and examples. This is on the condition that we obey Him immediately and completely, just as the paralytic and the centurion did.

[1] An unpublished note written around 1946.

5

The Gospel of Jesus has passages that are almost totally mysterious. We don't know how to integrate them into our lives. But there are others that are crystal clear. An innocent faithfulness to what we comprehend will lead us to understand what continues to be mysterious.

If we're called to simplify things that seem to us to be complicated, we're never, on the other hand, called to complicate things that are simple. When Jesus tells us to "lend without expecting any repayment," or "Let your 'Yes' mean 'Yes,' and your 'No' mean 'No.' Anything more is from the evil one," we're only asked to obey Him, and reasoning won't help us.

Carrying and keeping the Word we want to obey in the warmth of our faith and hope will help us. A kind of living pact of life will be established between this word and our will.

When we hold our Gospel in our hands, we should think that the Word lives in it. He wants to become flesh in us and take hold of us. This is so that with His heart, grafted onto our hearts, and His Spirit, connected to our spirits, we'll restart His life in another place, time, and human society.

Examining the Gospel in this way entails surrendering our lives in order to receive a destiny that's completely formed after Christ's likeness.

Why We Love Fr. Foucauld[2]

THE CONSIDERABLE INFLUENCE THAT "the man of the desert" had on our time has led to many contemporary vocations. The large synthesis that his life represented explains why such different paths can claim to be his. He's the meeting place of so many contrasts!

He had an uncontrollable need to pray to God and totally gave of himself to everyone who called upon him.

He ingeniously imitated Christ's life, gestures, and actions in Palestine, understood the people he was with, and adapted himself to them.

He had a passionate love for his next-door neighbor and a faithful love for all of humanity in every moment.

He so tenderly recreated the house in Nazareth around an exposed host, and walked across the tracks of the Sahara to consume one.

He was stubbornly heroic in a vocation that was roughly sketched and understood and prepared for other people's vocations.

---

[2]   This text appeared in *Vie Spirituelle* [*Spiritual Life*], November 1946.

He was devoted to manual labor and tirelessly persevered in scholarly work.

He had an incessant desire for a spiritual family and a divine vocation to a spiritual solitude that his death would complete.

How can we be astonished that so many gifted people who now give their lives to God have recognized their call and found a model in this life that was such a crossroads of graces?

Also, while allowing others to say how Fr. Foucauld enlightened, guided, or confirmed them on their path, we simply want to emphasize the aspects of his life that have helped us find ours.

In the Pure Loss of Oneself

Quoting Bossuet, Foucauld said: "To breathe before God in the pure loss of oneself." An extraordinary type of gratuitousness emerged in his whole life. God, if He was his God, always continued to be God. Foucauld loved Him first and foremost because He was God.

Charles de Foucauld is for us the model of those God-centered vocations that directly attract the soul for God in Christ. Those people don't have any choice. God is their whole horizon. He's eminently preferred because of the very fact that He exists.

> As soon as I understood that there was a God, I understood that I could only live for Him. My religious vocation dates from the same moment as my faith. God is so big. There's an unbridgeable difference between Him and everything that's not Him![3]

For these people, the love of Christ leads to the love of all our brothers and sisters, just as for others, the vocation to the apostolate is the path on which they give themselves completely to Christ.

[3]   *Lettres à H. de Castries*, 97.

This gratuitousness about God bore fruit in his relationships toward his neighbor. Charles de Foucauld offered him his life every day. We know how generous and available he was. He was ready to die for him and eventually did. He didn't wait for the results and wasn't disturbed about feeling like a complete failure. He remained at peace when, having spent practically his whole life in the desert, his only reward was the conversion of an African man and an elderly woman. These weren't guaranteed. He loved for the sake of loving because God is love and God was in him. He imitated his Lord as much as possible by loving all his loved ones.

This was because Fr. Foucauld, the man of adoration, was a man of solitude and of the desert. Wherever a man goes — even in a desert — man must make *his* desert.

Fr. Foucauld has enlightened us with a new clarity about God's first commandment to humanity: "You will adore one God."

Prayer has often been compared to breathing. Throughout the writings of Fr. Foucauld, prayer takes shape as a "weight" of the soul, like that action that puts a person face to face with his God in his human behavior. We think that this attitude of the creature toward his Creator is the one that's appropriate for us to urgently take in a world that's inverted toward man and diverted from his purpose. It's essential that many of us devote ourselves to this. The Mystical Body needs it.

At this time, the Holy Spirit is driving so many vocations toward the pursuit of lost people. So many Christians, who are driven by the love of Christ, are desperately looking at those who are lost in order to be all things to all people, except for sin; to meet them wherever they have been led astray. Others who are turned toward God are needed. People who adore are needed inside the human dough. These are people who are so convinced of the need for what they are doing that even if they are deprived of acting on behalf of their fellow humans, they know they are responding to the essential part of their vocation by repeating to God in our contemporary deserts, subways, roads, houses, and farms: "You're the one who is. We're the ones who aren't."

Our time needs these sacrifices that are undertaken among those who are unaware of them. It needs voices that "cry out in our deserts," a phrase common in Fr. Foucauld's writings and on which his life was centered: "We thank You because of Your great glory," "in the pure loss of ourselves."

The Universal Brother

Fr. Foucauld seems to us to be rooted at the crossroads of love. He loved everyone he saw. He brought together two opposite ends of love in his life — the next-door neighbor and the whole world.

He often said: "To be a tender brother." This word *tender* keeps recurring. It's full of human care. He also said: "to be a savior," which carried with it heavy connotations of redemption.

He deliberately settled into a genuine family life with every human being he encountered. This family life would be the necessary sign of another one of his family lives that continuously deepened day and night with everyone on earth.

Living this double family life would mean having stones put on sand as an enclosure. It would mean listening a lot and talking only a little. It would mean offering his food ration or a knitting lesson. It would mean bringing a Tuareg leader to France and being buried himself in Tamanrasset. It would mean collecting local poetry and nurturing others. It would mean living alone in the midst of Muslims and dying and being killed by them. It would mean giving everyone what he needed because Jesus was essentially the one who gave, and Charles of Jesus acted with Him and like Him. It would mean not having a schedule that would include what could and couldn't be done, but rather being for everyone what his "tender brother" would be. It would be seeing sinners as "foolish people" and keeping the warmest parts of one's heart for them. It would mean generously opening up to those who surrounded him, without letting them be attached to him. It would mean knowing that love bursts forth, explodes, and dispenses grace in the world through them.

"Lord, may everyone go to Heaven." This was the first prayer he planned to teach to the catechumens he'd never have. All the prayers and penances in the rule for the Little Brothers of the Sacred Heart were arranged for the intentions of the Sovereign Pontiff — that is to say, all of them were to have a worldwide dimension.

We've learned from Fr. Foucauld that in order to give ourselves to the entire world, we have to break through everything that binds us up in order for us to "set our hearts at large." It's not necessary to do this within the walls of a monastery. It can be done in an enclosure of dry stones that are laid on the sand. It can be in an African caravan. It can be in one of our homes, a workshop, a stairway that we're climbing, or a bus that we're taking. We set our hearts at large by accepting the narrow, constant enclosure of love of the next-door neighbor. Giving perfect love to those we approach, letting ourselves be enchained by this consuming dependence, and living the Sermon on the Mount as a matter of course is the door that sets our hearts at large — a narrow door that leads to universal love.

He taught us to be completely happy to be placed at a crossroads of life, to be ready to love those who go by and, through them, all those in the world who are suffering, lost, or living in darkness.

He explained to us that its sovereign effectiveness lay in its majestic gratuitousness, and that agreeing to see nothing about what we do, but to keep loving anyway, is the best way to save someone without fail anywhere on the earth.

The Heart That's Planted by the Cross

The heart that's planted with a cross has taught us that this total love is possible only at the cost of everything that seems negative and that is its underside, so to speak. This includes poverty, obedience, purity, and humility. All this negativity "makes us free to love." It's at the cost of what we could call negative, which is actually positive and better — namely, the cross. It's a voluntary participation in the Lord's Passion, regardless of whether it's physical or spiritual pain, suffering or humiliation, or, according to Foucauld's saying, deliberate shame. The heart planted in the cross in this area teaches us that all the reasons that the mind can offer us are worth little in the presence of the heart's reasons.

This cross was really the focus of his heart — the solid pivotal point around which his universal love fell into place. Without it, our love will remain indefinitely anemic, incomplete, and mutilated. Love that doesn't carry the cross inside it continually bumps into other crosses. It stumbles and crawls. Love that's connected to the cross has stepped over the obstacle as before.

"Jesus Caritas" is written above and below this heart and cross. Love without suffering remains our love. Saving love — the love of Jesus — is love that suffers. He accomplished His redemption through suffering — through this discernible good. The heart that's planted in the cross is a heart that goes further than suffering that comes on its own. It goes further than the suffering that is connected to everything that's poor, humble, and obedient. It even goes so far as to desire suffering.

"When we can suffer and love, we can do a lot. We can do the most that we can in this world."

These words are those of Fr. Foucauld. He wrote them on December 1, 1916, the day of his death. They are a response to those who — in our time — still speak of the scandal of the Cross and are embarrassed by a Christianity that entails suffering and being counted as worthless.

Exclaiming the Gospel with One's Life

"Ask yourself about everything: 'What would the Lord have done?' Then do it. It's your only rule, but it's your absolute rule."

Charles de Foucauld is a real contemporary of Jesus of Nazareth in the middle of the twentieth century. He imitated Him in a rustic and meticulous way. He contemplated Him by deliberately settling into the midst of the apostles — "between the Blessed Virgin Mary and St. Mary Magdalen." He wanted to become one of the Master's close friends and blended in with their lives. He carefully listened to the Lord's teachings while going over all of His Word with a fine-tooth comb to obey it to the last detail. This is the imitation that was never fulfilled which led him to the priesthood.

In looking at Charles de Foucauld, we learn about this child obeying the evangelical message. This was a trusting obedience that didn't ask for any explanations. He obeyed — not because of what was being commanded, but because of the one who was commanding.

The Gospel was his whole visible apostolate. He gave his brothers an illustrated edition of this Gospel. He thought these images from life were the best conveyance of grace. In seeing him embody each line of the Gospel in himself, we have understood that what people needed was to read the Gospel and watch it being experienced. The apostles preached and experienced their whole message — the beatitude of poverty along with the others. Doesn't our failure to spread the gospel come from separating preaching from life — our word from our example?

All the power of simplicity emerged for us from this evangelical life. It has shown us that it's possible for a Christian human spirit to put us on equal terms with every human being we meet. Fr. Foucauld revived Jesus of Palestine's figure of brotherly love for us. He welcomed all who crossed his path in his heart — workers and scholars, Jews and foreigners, the sick and children. He was so simple that everyone could interpret him.

He taught us that, besides necessary apostolates that require that the apostle must take on the environment in which he has to evangelize and almost espouse it, there's another apostolate that requires that we simplify our whole being. This entails rejecting everything we've acquired, our entire social selves, and acquiring a poverty that's a little dizzying. This kind of evangelical or apostolic poverty makes one totally flexible to connect with our brother in any situation without having any innate or acquired baggage that prevents us from running toward him. It asks the question about everything to everyone alongside the specialized apostolate.

Charles de Foucauld was the friend of every passerby, soldier, scholar, and doctor while living in the heart of the desert, buried among Muslims. He knew how to mingle with someone like General Laperinne and helped get beyond pigeonholing people in order for our lives to become a universal message that everyone can understand.

The Last Place

"Christ took the last place to such an extent that nobody could take it away from Him."

It's with this remark by Fr. Huvelin, which was "inviolably etched on the soul" of Fr. Foucauld, that we end this reflection.

He understood with his entire soul — and he helps us understand — that we can be truly intimate with Christ if we join the place that is His, which is the last one. It has helped us lose faith in prestige and acquire the Faith through our own self-erasure. It purifies our idea of witnessing all that could involve a "billboard" dimension, according to the phrase of a priest who understood it well. It has taught us that if some of us are taught to be in charge of temporal things or be responsible for doing good things, in the spirit of Christ, others are called to bury themselves in the last place for the simple goal of sharing it with Him. Fr. Foucauld placed the image of the Holy Face in front of the *unique model*, where only the phrases from the Gospel have been written — the Christ of insults, ridicule, abandonment, and failures. It's the very last place. *Sicut Deus delixit nos* is highlighted in writing. "So, God wants us to love Him" fills all of Charles of Jesus' life.

Joys Coming from the Mountain[4]

BECAUSE YOUR WORDS, MY God, aren't made to remain lifeless in our books, but to own us and go around the world in us, allow this fire of joy, which was previously lit by You on a mountain, to enrapture us. Grant that from this lesson on happiness, sparks would reach us, bite us, flood us, and overwhelm us, so that like "flames in the stubble" we would rush through the streets of the city, walk into the teeming crowds, and spread this infection of bliss and joy.

For we have had enough of all these heralds of bad and sad news. They make so much noise that Your Word no longer resounds. May the exciting silence of Your message shatter their noise.

Make the joy that we've received go into the faceless mob. May it be more resounding than the cries of the newspaper sellers — more pervasive than the contagious sadness of the masses.

Blessed Are the Poor in Spirit

... for the Kingdom of God is theirs.

Being poor isn't attractive. All poor people know this.

---

[4]   Published in *Études carmélitaines* [*Carmelite Studies*], August – September, 1947.

Possessing the Kingdom is attractive, but only the poor possess it.

Don't think that our joy consists of spending our days emptying our hands, heads, and hearts. Our joy consists of spending our days carving a place in our hands, heads, and hearts for the Kingdom of God that's passing by.

For it's amazing to know that God is so close to us. It's tremendous to know that it's possible for His love to be in us and upon us, and not open this one simple door of spiritual poverty for Him.

When your belongings leave at God's discretion, speak no longer of poverty, but of wealth.

Like a blind person who is being returned to his homeland, without seeing, then inhale the Kingdom's climate, warm yourselves up in its invisible sun, and feel the warm earth under your feet.

Don't say: "I've lost everything." Say instead: "I've gained everything."

Don't say: "They're taking everything from me." Say instead: "I'm receiving everything."

To meet Him, start your day without any preconceived ideas or anticipated weariness, without plans or memories about God, and without enthusiasm or a set of preconceived notions.

Leave without a road map to discover Him, knowing that He's found along the way and not at the end.

Don't try to find Him with original formulas; let yourself be found by Him in the poverty of a common life.

Monotony is poverty. Accept it.

Don't look for beautiful imaginary trips.

Let the varieties of the Kingdom of God be enough for you and let them delight you.

Lose interest in your health, for worrying about it is a luxury. Old age will teach you about birth and the death of resurrection.

Time will seem to you to be a little fold in the vastness of eternity.

You'll judge everything according to its eternal traces.

If you love the Kingdom of Heaven, you'll rejoice that your understanding is at a loss in the face of the divine, and you'll try to have more faith.

If your prayer is stripped of tender emotions, you'll know that God isn't reached through your nerves.

If you're not very courageous, you'll rejoice that you'll be suited for hope.

If you find that people are boring and that your heart is miserable, you'll be happy to have that imperceptible charity in you.

When you're depleted of everything, and you only see a house that's been emptied in the world, and poverty without a facade in you, think of the shadowy eyes that are open in the center of your soul, attached to inexpressible things, because the Kingdom of God is within you.

Blessed Are the Peacemakers

... for they shall be called children of God.

There are minor wars at all street corners, just as there are major wars in all the corners of the world.

We can make war or peace at each of the turning points in our lives.

We feel that we're dangerously built to make war.

Our neighbor very quickly becomes our enemy if he's not our brother.

When friends' possessions are placed next to each other, it often leads to irritation, whereas all of God's children manage and share their Father's possessions.

This is why only God's children are totally peaceful.

For them, the earth is their Heavenly Father's house.

Everything that's on earth is His, including the ground itself.

Yes, the earth is really one of our Heavenly Father's little homes.

They don't despise any room, continent, tiny island, nation, small courtyard, square, sidewalk, office, store, platform, or railroad station.

They have to cultivate the family spirit there.

While going on the road each morning, they marvel at getting to know all those brothers with their eyes of flesh that they had from the outset only met in the depth of faith. They can neither isolate themselves from them nor treat them as strangers. The right to a seat becomes debatable, and commercial ownership becomes much less uncompromising.

Social distinctions become tenuous.

The categories of human values become tenuous.

Few differences hold up in front of this common title of sons and daughters of God. They're not any more important or visible than a dyed thread on the entire surface of a white sheet.

Just as we can see clothes, muscles, and everything that's not the main part of an organism disappear on an X-ray screen, everything that's not part of our theological kinship in the presence of this title of sons of God disappears.

Peacemakers' eyes are kind, and their companions warm up beside them, as they do at the fireside. They never find a reason to fight because they know they are only accountable for peace, and peace doesn't defend itself through battles.

They know that dividing a single atom can unleash cosmic wars.

They also know there's a chain that connects humans together and that when a human cell is torn by rage, resentment, or bitterness, the catalyst of war can rebound to the end of the universe.

But because they believe in spreading love, they know that when a little peace is created, there's a spillover of peace that's strong enough to fill the whole world.

They also go into a twofold joy — that of bringing peace all around them and that of hearing an inexpressible voice that says "Father" in the depths of their hearts.

Blessed Are the Merciful

... for they will obtain mercy.

Being merciful doesn't seem like a very restful job.

It's bad enough to suffer from your own miseries without having to endure the pain of others.

Our heart would refuse to do so if there were other ways of receiving mercy.

So, let's not complain too much if we often have tears in our eyes when we see so much pain.

We know God's tenderness through them.

Just as solid melting pots are needed to carry liquid metal, which is completely possessed and worked on by the fire, so God needs solid hearts where our seven miseries, in search of healing and the eternal mercy, yearning to be redeemed, can live together.

If our heart is often disgusted by so closely touching this mass of misery — not ever knowing if it's our own or someone else's — we wouldn't want to change this task for anything in the world, because we find our joy in being close to this relentless fire that endlessly proves God's love.

We've gotten so used to this presence of fire that we spontaneously go looking for all those who can allow it to burn — all those who are little and weak, who moan and suffer, who sin, crawl, fall, and need to be healed.

In communion with this fire that burns in us, we offer to Him all these distressed people whom we've met so that He can touch and heal them.

Blessed Are the Meek

... for they will inherit the earth.

Being meek is accepting Your visit to us — without preconditions and without any kinks.

This involves offering You a heart that's really free of habits and preferences, and so united to Your goodwill that Your actions come about in it without encountering any resistance.

For what You need to accomplish Your work on earth isn't so much our sensational actions, but a certain amount of submission, a certain degree of surrender, and a certain weight of blind abandonment that can be found anywhere in a crowd of people.

If all this weight of abandonment, submission, and surrender was united in a single heart, the shape of the world would surely change.

For this lone heart would let You go by, would be the breach for an invasion, and the weak point where the universal revolt would concede.

It takes a long time to have a gentle heart.

It's done minute by minute, second by second, and day by day.

Just as the thread of soft and supple wool makes the sweater on the needles that guide it — stitch by stitch — so our heart's fibers mellow and soften over the movement of Your will.

In this conversation where our silence receives other people's remarks or our thoughts yield to other people's thoughts, in those lifeless things that seem to want to strike us — our pen that writes poorly, the heat that tires us, the cold that numbs us; in those judgments about us in which we hardly recognize our appearance; in those small or large pains that lurk inside us — along our nerves — let us let our lives unfold.

Let the minutes lengthen, one after the other — stitch by stich — in the providential thread in which You enfold everything that is Yours.

Blessed Are the Pure of Heart

… for they will see God.

You've told us, Lord, that we wouldn't be able to see You in this unrelenting purity.

Since we've known it, we've found ourselves loving it, as we love that which leads to what we love.

For our love is bored with these delays that shield You from us and this slowness that indefinitely postpones our being able to encounter Your face.

We know that purity will loosen thousands of these hands that grip us, exhaust us, hinder us, and interrupt us.

It's freedom from every stoppage, being possessed by nothing, being able to go toward You all at once.

It's an urgent, impatient, intrusive love that doesn't tolerate nuisances.

This is why its last assault will be at the hour of our death.

It will make us climb aboard this spiritual train that will take us beyond ourselves.

Everything will wave goodbye through the windows.

Not one of them will offer to climb on with us.

All of them will be afraid to accompany us.

They will all seem temporary to us — without any value except as a stopover.

We'll leave everything. Everything will leave us.

We'll be confined in an irresistible momentum.

The only thing that will count for us and will interest us is that last turn of the wheel and this abrupt stop without a departure in the land of eternity before the God who waits for us whom we'll see when the basic purity of death will lead us to Him after the patient purity of our life.

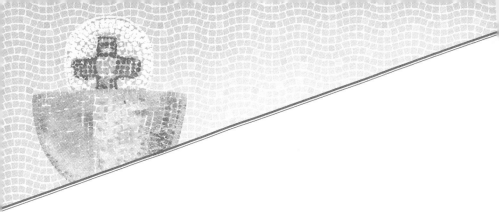

The Love of God Translated[5]

IF WE MAKE OURSELVES totally available to the Lord's tasks — tasks that His glory, love, and mercy lead to — we'll be immersed into a mystery where our logical reasoning is short-lived, and our understanding must know how to become blind.

When this time we can't foresee comes, we have only one unfailing light. This unfailing light helps us live and act in the often confusing but very clear context of constant or temporary circumstances. This light is the Gospel of Jesus Christ, which is given to us by the Church, along with her commentary.

[5] This text from 1956, like many of those published in this volume, was written for the group in which Madeleine Delbrêl lived from 1933 to 1964. She'd provided the momentum to start this group with Fr. Lorenzo, and she kept leading it until her death. We've extracted what we think could help every Christian live the gospel from these notes, which were written by laypeople who wanted to experience the evangelical counsels as a team. Incidentally, Delbrêl often expanded her thoughts beyond the people she was directly addressing. If she sometimes used the feminine form, she most often wrote in the masculine form. This alternation has been respected.

To hear it, Jesus expects us to have children's ears, which don't add to or take away anything from what they hear. Then, they do it the way they heard it.

But children can understand in different ways that complement each other, while sometimes contradicting each other. This is why we must understand how wise the Church is in not taking her eyes off her children.

Only the Church watches over the Gospel. It has the continual right to watch over the interpretation which is publicly given.

This right is even a duty. For this Gospel which, along with the Body of Christ, is undoubtedly its greatest treasure, has truly aroused, guided, and promoted many great saints. But it's also true that it's provided many heresies, both major and minor, with the vigor that every truth that's been led astray preserves.

So, everything that we've received from the Gospel as vital instruction must be listed while we're searching for the watching Church.

Certain conditions are required of us, and Jesus has explained most of them.

⊹ The Lord's words form a whole. They don't break apart. If we experience one of them more, it must not be to the detriment of another one.
⊹ We have to *keep* these words. They must remain in us. We have to read or listen to them in order to know them. But whether they are read or understood, they must be carried in us just as the earth carries the seed. As they are carried, they have to sprout and bear fruit in us. We can't always read them quickly.

These words are spoken in human tongues and often speak of human actions. We can only *keep* those we understand and forget those we must believe . . . whereas the Gospel leads us to true supernatural life. Jesus holds both ends. He speaks of the drink given to the thirsty, which will have its reward — a gift so mundane that even a plant would be happy with it. And when the price of men's salvation is so costly, blood is shed … for a God who remains mysterious.

All that seems to even out for the Lord whose love changes everything into gold. He won't evaluate the weight of our loving acts, but instead the love that made us act.

Simply and promptly submitting to Jesus' words and examples will be a firm rope on the great chasm of charity for us. We'll be able to see its human side, but we will only be able to believe its divine side.

By constantly reading the Gospel in a way that isn't closed off, and taking it up as if from scratch, we're asking for a point of contact with a word of life that makes it possible for this word to go everywhere in us as far as it wants to go. There's always an "end point of the world" in each one of us.

If each point has its secondary methods, I think the main point is letting the Gospel form us in Christ's image as we prayerfully and realistically absorb it. It's in the Gospel that it will be proven to us how the love of God "made flesh" can spell each letter of the two great commandments, and it is there that we'll see how love for our God — if this love is as great as we can make it — not only can but *must* involve loving people from everywhere and at all times — loving everyone whose destiny crosses ours, with a capacity to sacrifice, the energy to act, and the strength to "bear" suffering that isn't in proportion to the measures we know how to take and the values we esteem.

Without the Gospel, how could we have understood that St. John's "God is love" wasn't only an astounding and adorable mystery? The itinerary of this God-Love had been narrated to us up to the very limits of our flesh, in order for us to, in turn, redo the same itinerary the other way, and end up, not in the middle of the night, but in the fullness of truth in the mystery of God's love.

By showing us God made flesh and by repeating what He said to people, the Gospel teaches us that the love of God loves simply because He is love — in the way a poor person loves. It also teaches us how He loves everyone, not because everyone is lovable, but because He's invincibly loving.

If He seems to have preferences, they are the reverse of all attractions. What we repel and say is evil is for Him the lack of something good. He rushes over to nourish it, heal it, revive it, forgive it, or convert it — to evangelize and redeem all of us because we're all affected by the same evil.

The Gospel makes us climb over the words *active, contemplative,* and *apostolic* to meet the one whose reflection they are: Jesus Christ.

We meet Him just for a moment. For the Gospel also teaches us that we lose Him as soon as we stop even for the time to catch our breath. His love is a continuous movement. "Come ... Follow me ... Go ..."

Even those we think were sedentary must walk. A man climbs in a tree to see Him. He's told to hurry to come down from it and go back home. That's where Jesus will meet him.

Hastily — He only has three years for this work — Jesus chooses His twelve men. He teaches them what this choice has done to them.

- ✠ Heralds of the Gospel — the good news.
- ✠ Images of the Gospel — men to whom God has given His love to love Him with.
- ✠ People who are finally forced to experience the three counsels because of God's love.

Love pushes them like an unknown wind. They are unaware of where they are going. This happens to a lot of other people, but they "no longer know where they are coming from" — and that's much rarer. To find the lost, it's almost always necessary to risk losing your way back home. They are possessed by the new life they are announcing, which is forming them even as they continue to be grafted onto their risen Lord, who is present and will be present to them up until the end of time.

Through them, He still wants His favorite people — those from the entire world — as well as everyone else to hear the announcement of eternal life.

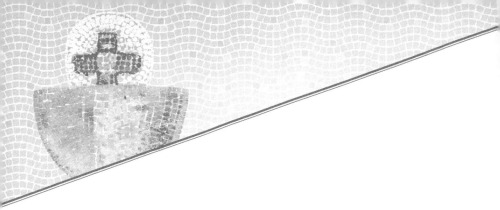

A Voice That Exclaimed the Gospel[6]

Fr. Lorenzo

FR. LORENZO DIED A little more than a year ago. He collapsed in the subway on the feast of the Epiphany while he was reciting the Divine Office. He was neck and neck with the crowd. His death, which occurred a few minutes later, took up about as much space as it did time.

---

[6]   Elsewhere, Madeleine Delbrêl wrote about Fr. Lorenzo: "He made the Gospel explode for me. Instead of simply being the book in which the God we proclaim was adored, contemplated, and revealed, the Gospel has become something more. It has become the book that, in the Church's hands, tells us how to live for contemplation, how to live to adore while adoring, and how to live by listening to the good news and proclaiming it. The Gospel has become, not only the book of the living Lord, but also the Lord's book to live by." Fr. Lorenzo, along with Delbrêl, was the originator of the common life group that she lived in until she died. He was ordained as a priest in 1921. He was named as the pastor of Sts. Peter and Paul in Ivry in 1934. He became the co-director of the French mission seminary in 1942. Then, he was the pastor of St. Hippolytus Church in Paris in 1945. He was the chaplain for the retreat house in Bagneux when God suddenly called him back to Himself on January 6, 1958, as he was saying his breviary in a crowded subway. It was the office for the Epiphany. These notes were published in the *Lettres aux communautés de la mission de France* in the August – September 1959 issue.

Three quarters of his work was done. His death could come quickly and at no cost. For, before he died, Fr. Lorenzo had disappeared in many ways. His life had patiently made him do this. Hardly anything remained in him besides what was eternal — his priestly love for Jesus Christ and the Gospel. His whole life had become its voice.

God allowed his death to authenticate his life briefly and publicly.

The priest who "passionately loved Jesus Christ" died as a priest while reciting the priestly prayer underneath the streets that were home to one of his former parishes. He was clad in his priestly clothes and rested for several days in the midst of those who were suffering in the hospital. Priest as he was, he didn't leave Paris without the Mass being celebrated for him at Notre-Dame, where he was happy to be a canon. This is how he shared in Paris's public prayer.

He was able to experience the Gospel to the end, which he said could be experienced everywhere. Jesus, "the poor man who was born on the wood and died on the wood," let Fr. Lorenzo imitate Him in a folksy way that Fr. Lorenzo loved. A seat in the subway was a little bit like a cross for him.

Fr. Lorenzo could still obey the Gospel commandment he wanted to give everyone — to love those we know and don't know — by offering his life among the people he met.

The following notes say only a little about Fr. Lorenzo. Their intention is to focus on what Fr. Lorenzo's proclamation of the Gospel was for me and many others.

A Priest

We can say this about Fr. Lorenzo: "He wanted to be a priest and nothing more." He wanted to be a priest in a common and simple way. What was essential in every priest's life seems to have been sufficient and excessive for him.

He was most often satisfied in taking on what was proper in the different jobs that were entrusted to him and doing it in a perfect and ordinary way. So, when the Assembly of Cardinals and Archbishops initiated the French mission in cities and regions where the lack of priests preceded or followed their dechristianization, Fr. Lorenzo went there. It was part of the logic of his priesthood.

He brought a vocation to the seminary in Lisieux. Its extreme simplicity was providentially adapted to what was germinating there. But later, it became partially distinct from what the French Mission was seeking, testing, and choosing in its time of growth.

This tension would necessarily emerge in the logic of the two vocations.

These successive portraits of the young Fr. Lorenzo would undoubtedly be possible. From a rather remote period — around that of his transition to Notre-Dame-des-Champs — these successive portraits would undoubtedly only be repetitions of a single portrait that was more and more simple. For, if Fr. Lorenzo naturally had a uniquely original personality, he agreed to have it whittle away so well through contact with circumstances that almost nothing remained from this initial uniqueness. That's probably what was surprising about him when he died.

We could trace a priestly portrait of Fr. Lorenzo — the "man of God" that he was and remained in everything, with his free ambition of a "loyal and full priesthood," his rejection of every personal interest to accept only what God wanted, the unity of an existence whose priesthood remained the only reason for being and the only goal — even the love of God that his simple life didn't manage to hide, and his tenderness for Christ that modeled so many of his actions. We could say all that, but we'd know that other priests have experienced this kind of life, are living it, or will live it among us. Others besides him had his cordial kindness toward people who were grieving. Others heard confessions as he heard them, and gave the sinner all the love of their souls and all the warmth of their hearts because of their own sins. Do we need to speak about this?

It was enough to have heard Fr. Lorenzo say almost every time he mentioned Christ's friendship: "Behold, I am standing at the door, knocking. If one of you hears my voice and opens the door, I will come in and dine with that person, and that person with me," to have sensed that a unique intimacy existed between the Lord Jesus and Fr. Lorenzo. But do we have the right to suggest something that he passed over in silence?

However, before this life that deters words, we still have a right to speak. It's a right that's perhaps a sort of duty — the right to say what some people received from Fr. Lorenzo, because this seems to have been his own mission. We have to say that a voice called the Gospel out to us, and that thanks to it, we've heard the Gospel as a message that directly targeted us, as a present-day and a personal call, and that Fr. Lorenzo — body and soul — was this voice.

The Gospel

"This seducer." Taking up the old accusation that was hurled against Jesus, Fr. Lorenzo loved to provoke the Lord in this way with a tone of joyful defeat. He said: "We don't resist His love, and yet, it's a totalitarian love."

Fr. Lorenzo's life was an apostolic life only and simply because it was a priestly life. If it was, moreover, missionary — in a very precise and particular sense of this word — it was because he made this phrase of St. Paul his own: "Woe to me if I fail to proclaim the Gospel!" Woe to him, for his deep conviction was that when we know Jesus Christ, we love Him. But how will they love Him if the Gospel isn't announced to them? Also, many of us respond to this: "Woe is me." This response is one of gratitude: "Blessed are those who hear the Word of God" and try to keep it.

Among those who "heard" the Gospel in this way, some had received the Faith before knowing Fr. Lorenzo. Others had received and kept it since they were children. Few had received it while they were meeting with Fr. Lorenzo. But the kind of conversion that occurred most frequently in his presence and as an immediate result of contact with him was the St. John the Baptist kind of conversion. So many of us were deeply moved by what he himself liked to call the *metanoia* — this turnaround — this conversion caused by the irruption of the Lord's word in our lives. It was a word that was addressed to us on that very day. The Lord Jesus, so alive that He could speak to them and call each one of them, also asks, demands, advises, and leads us.

Fr. Lorenzo didn't speak about the Lord. He said: "The Lord says this. The Lord asks that. The Lord doesn't want this. The Lord wants you like that." Father didn't say this with his own words. No. We heard: "The Lord says this to you. The Lord calls you like that. He tells you what He's always said. He calls you as He's always called you." Then he'd say: "Look at the Lord in His Word. He tells you what He is. Look." He concluded with some saint's words — "Nothing is better than God, who is so good," "A person is too greedy if God isn't enough" — or by some foregone conclusions that were his own: "We're tremendously loved," "The Lord has loved us at a great cost; we can't love Him on the cheap," and "We can't love God with leftovers." But these were only exclamations of someone who, while repeating the Lord's words, had listened to them at the same time as us.

"... And to Every Creature."

The light with which the Church illuminates the Lord's words reaches everyone differently, although it remains singular for all of them. That is why "preaching the Gospel to every creature" today means — for some — going toward a race or class. For others, it means staying in their own class or race. For Fr. Lorenzo, "preaching to every creature" was preaching to those who were in front of him. He didn't choose them, and the Lord hadn't designated them for him ahead of time. "A man was going down from Jericho." In order to be a good Samaritan of the Word, Fr. Lorenzo didn't ask himself if this person was Jewish, or if he was attractive or repugnant. What repelled him was the distinction people made between human beings, whatever their distinctions were. A person was a person. He even refused to put people into categories, which were snider than classes or races — people who were gifted or not gifted, boring or brilliant, intelligent or not very intelligent, charming or repulsive. Everyone in Fr. Lorenzo's audiences found himself to be personally targeted and "invited" by the speaker. They were often made up of all ages, from completely different "worlds." However many people were there, everyone discovered or learned more concretely that he was called "by his name," and because he was a person himself, he could respond "My Lord and my God," and that an assembly of brothers and sisters could say "Our Father" because everyone was loved for himself like no other.

"... They Departed for Their Own Country by Another Route."

When Fr. Lorenzo preached about the Epiphany, he always insisted on this "other path from which we return from having encountered the Lord."

The Gospel that Fr. Lorenzo preached lacked commentaries. We can't even say that he drew any conclusions from it. People's personal applications and deep resolutions were reactions, which suited them through a powerful contact with the Word of Jesus Christ. The way in which Fr. Lorenzo transmitted this word, his infinite respect for it, and the love he put into pronouncing the words provoked a sudden awareness of an event. It was important that none of it was lost.

We understood that if God took the trouble to speak to us in our own language, if He wanted the way he spoke things to come to us, and if He had selected things that had to be transmitted from one century to another, it was because they were all crucial. They could only be an invaluable treasure since they were given by Him. We understood what an amazing privilege we were rewarded with by being so "amicably" able to access — without their being a need for miracles — the thoughts, feelings, and desires of the living God — to be able to listen to this living God and look at Him in His Word. In the past, you couldn't look at Him without dying. But afterward, there was no way to avoid realizing that Jesus Christ, the Son of God, had spoken to us.

Fr. Lorenzo demonstrated the commandments, advice, and calls that the Lord had clearly and simply given — which he had exemplified — with the same simplicity. Thus, this new path opened up before each one of us. We undoubtedly remained free to commit to it or not. But suddenly this freedom could only seem to be used in order to walk, because walking meant walking side by side, heart to heart, and one on one with the Lord. We could also say hand to hand, for this path of light continuously sprang from the eucharistic mystery and continually dove back into it. Likewise, a human path wasn't the only thing that remained. It was "another path" that was rooted in the living darkness of faith and that went from "clarity to clarity" toward the mysteries of eternal life.

"... The Lord Is Calling You."

When Fr. Lorenzo talked about Christ, he most often said "the Lord Jesus." The Gospel is the Lord Jesus making Himself known. We could love the Lord Jesus in the Gospel. We could love Him with all of the earth's passion and all of Heaven's love.

The Lord Jesus was our God and Savior. Being Lord, He had "all the rights." Being the Savior, He had all mercies. We'd be permanently poor in front of this Savior.

Belonging to God made a person glorious. The one who belonged to Him was happy. But how were we to belong to Him? Fr. Lorenzo didn't worry about this too much. He trusted the Lord to make Himself understood by everyone. He was suspicious of man-made vocations — even if they were made by priests. As long as the love of the Lord Jesus was in someone's life, Jesus would create his personal vocation in it. I don't know if there's a single Christian to whom Fr. Lorenzo hadn't given this phrase from St. Thérèse of Lisieux as a "directive": "My vocation is love." When the Lord Jesus had given His explanation and when a particular person had understood what He wanted — a marriage, a monastery, the priesthood, or a chosen or authorized celibacy — Fr. Lorenzo then got out of his invincible silence and spoke of this vocation as if it were the only vocation in the world.

This is why those who had "unconditionally given themselves to the Lord Jesus" around Fr. Lorenzo ended up in an astonishing variety of callings.

After a sermon, days of recollection, or retreats, everyone left to where his appointed meeting was — to elderly people in a hospice, sick people in a little town, a Carmel in China, the Poor Clares in Assisi, black people in Africa, the end of the world or of his own world, a boy or girl that he loved, parents who couldn't be left alone, children who were always more numerous, or a childless home.

Fr. Lorenzo had sown the evangelical seed in everyone. He prayed that it would rain on hard soil and that the weeds wouldn't choke the good seed. For some, it was "go to the end of the world." For others, it was "Zacchaeus, I'm going to eat at your house tonight."

"What Do You Have That You Haven't Received?"

Fr. Lorenzo's dark little silhouette, which was sometimes thinned down and sometimes heavy, would have signified humility by itself if humility could have a sign. I can't remember this silhouette in my heart without seeing again what it so revealed without his knowing it. It was a poverty that was continually more hollowed out and less defined — a poverty that was nothing more than the weight and place of the gospel in Fr. Lorenzo's entire being.

The gospel didn't belong to him, but he belonged to the gospel because he belonged to Christ. Because he was an "ambassador who was charged with connections," the gospel dwelt freely in him. Because he wanted everyone to be free to receive the whole gospel, he was the captive ambassador of all those to whom he should announce it. This is how its message always hollowed out more of a poverty within him.

The gospel belonged to the Lord and, as such, to all people. Fr. Lorenzo didn't think he had the right to alter it like *this* for some and like *that* for others. He didn't think there was one gospel for the poor and another one for the rich — a gospel for the powerful and a gospel for the oppressed. He refused to make any kinds of special editions of it, with certain texts for these people and others for those people.

There was a case where Fr. Lorenzo had a hard time keeping calm. It was when the gospel that he was so devoted to, and which he completely served, was used for something other than what God intended. It was when the gospel was used in the service of a human cause — even if this cause was great. Father then stood up as if someone's honor was at stake, and he could be almost harsh.

In choosing Fr. Lorenzo to proclaim His gospel, the Lord had chosen "what was weak." Alongside Fr. Lorenzo, we could easily be unaware of how strong this weakness had become. Courage was needed in order to be the simple messenger of a message from which nothing should be taken away and to which nothing should be added. For it continued to be more obvious that the mission he'd received was a lonely one. He had to experience it faithfully and alone. It remained firm in Fr. Lorenzo, who willingly refused to struggle and was so suspicious of what he was worth.

"... You Are Unprofitable Servants"

In relation to the Holy Gospel, people and things were for Fr. Lorenzo servants, but Fr. Lorenzo considered himself to be the lowest of servants. There was a whole category of methods for which Fr. Lorenzo didn't hide his skepticism or mistrust. He called these "techniques." He gave this word a meaning that was completely personal for him. Techniques included yesterday's methods and today's theories, specialized research, the worries of the temporal realm, and the struggles against sociological obstacles or psychological misunderstandings.

People, their worth, and even the witness of their lives were unprofitable servants. Of course, Fr. Lorenzo didn't mean that we were to be the messengers of the gospel without being its disciples. But he was very suspicious about using the word "witness." For him, the witness of a person's life was the witness it gave of the love for God. This witness played an efficacious role in the Redemption's profound economy. The fact of evangelizing was a secondary witness. For Fr. Lorenzo, the real witness was Jesus Christ, who testified about Himself in the Gospel. Above all, witnessing was repeating what Jesus, "the faithful witness," had said.

This sense of the unprofitable servant explains a whole other aspect of Fr. Lorenzo's character — namely, conforming his life to Jesus Christ's priesthood. Christ made him a spiritual father because the priest has to be a father, a master because the priest must be a master, and a guide because the priest must be a guide. But all this was a part of the priest — this "other Jesus Christ." It was immersed into the mystery of the grace of the priesthood.

On the other hand, what was visible in him and suitable for him was that his mission as a messenger made him continually repeat: "You have but one father who brings down every perfect gift and one master — the Master, and one guide — the one of whom Joan of Arc said: 'I think Jesus Christ and His Church are one.'"

Priests have said words like this, which didn't prevent them from being spiritual directors, trainers of the will, or leaders. On the contrary, Fr. Lorenzo really didn't correspond to any of that. He avoided these titles, tasks, and functions. A ready-made word doesn't define what he was for many of us.

I mentioned John the Baptist earlier. I'm coming back to him and will do so again. In order to give a glimpse of Fr. Lorenzo's role in our encounter with the Lord, I don't think we can do better than quote John the Baptist's last testimony: "It is the bridegroom who has the bride, but the friend of the bridegroom who stands by and listens for him rejoices greatly when he hears the bridegroom's voice. This joy of mine is complete. He must increase; I must decrease."

A Voice That Cries Out in the Desert

By nature, Fr. Lorenzo loved solitude. By nature, he was also rather fiercely individualistic. Yet I don't think he would have preferred to choose the solitude that the Lord had dedicated to him. He had willingly created some protected areas of his life for silence, prayer, and a kind of withdrawal, which allowed him to keep part of himself from those who were closest to him. But it wasn't so much by preference as by grace that he found himself alone. It was actually Fr. Lorenzo's own gift of grace that isolated him, above all.

I don't want to generalize, but I can't refrain from noting here what often struck me. Those to whom he seemed to be the most connected, either by the essential priesthood that he shared with them or the pure evangelism which he'd brought to them, were often distanced from him as a result of the very thing he'd given them. The grace whose instrument he had been often became an expansive energy in them, whereas when he received the same grace for himself, it increased his focus and deepened the power of his inner life. He rejoined the world through this immersion into God's mystery. But the spiritual journeys of those who rejoined this same world by gravitating to its surface became difficult for him to understand, even if they were obeying the initial impulse that the Father let them receive. This was how some of his family and friends became distant from him without being ungrateful. He suffered as a result.

God's love was freedom and solitude for him. Let's say more — solitude alone could bring freedom to love for Fr. Lorenzo. Therefore, inviting others to God's love was inviting them to solitude at the same time. What I said a little earlier explains why those who were called to the love of God by Fr. Lorenzo really heard a voice that was crying out in the desert, that was calling them from the desert and to the desert.

This wasn't a poetic desert. The one who continually returned to it to look for the Lord's instructions — as all God's messengers did — never made trips to the world's famous deserts. He rarely took trips to a Trappist or some other monastery. But solitude dwelt within him, and it sometimes pushed and sometimes pulled him to practice it modestly in his church, chapel, or room. It prompted him to continue this life of his that was a bit nomadic and constantly on the move. This is how he came to take this subway where he died, on these streets and on these trains, with their brief distances between stops, to connect with the ears of those who were to hear him, to have people within earshot.

But solitude accompanied him everywhere. It was a constitutive part of his being. It didn't let him go. It was in the solitude that God — through him — made an appointment for us. Fr. Lorenzo encouraged us to join him for this appointment. But once we were there, we perceived — more or less late and more or less completely — that Fr. Lorenzo had left and had left us alone with his Lord, who provided us with everything. And just now, as we were talking about false ingratitude, we're talking here about his false indifference. It wasn't that he didn't really value people. He thought he had only a small part to play in this intimate encounter with the Lord.

This is why — once he had made his Lord known — when our access to God was established, Fr. Lorenzo withdrew. We didn't always understand it very well. But before his death for some, and after his death for others, it became clear for many people "that it was good for him to leave" — even before the last departure.

To try to love God more than anything, we, one day or another, have to be forced to love God alone … and not His friends along with Him. So, we resigned ourselves to this or we accepted it, but we knew once and for all what it means to "prefer."

Fr. Lorenzo *forced* people to make this choice. I'm not even sure he did it on purpose.

Once this face to face meeting with God was established "in the shade," Fr. Lorenzo didn't lose interest in the person. He "abandoned" him. He abandoned us as long as we didn't have the Faith to abandon ourselves. He surrendered everyone into God's hands. Each person stayed there without knowing where to go. And God was free to act alone, so that everyone would become free for Him.

Because for Fr. Lorenzo, each person's sanctification, vocation, and mission were divine matters, where God should be free to operate and where God should find us free.

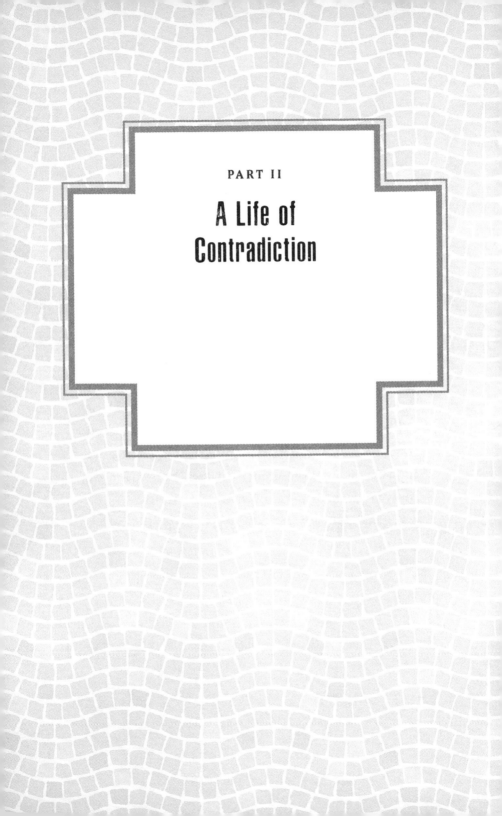

PART II

A Life of Contradiction

"The obligation to announce the good news is going to force us to walk in step with God and ourselves at the same time. This will most often give us the unusual gait of a lame person or the hesitant gait of a half blind person. With all our powers, spirit, and heart, we'll evangelize by applying Jesus Christ's program. But this program that we know immerses us completely into a plan that remains obscure for us. We don't know what the Lord will do with our everyday work, even if it's perfect. And if it's very imperfect or clumsy, we don't know any more about what it will be used for. We only know that what is given to God isn't lost."

Unpublished text, 1962.

To Love a Lot

Virtues Gone Mad[7]

SOMEONE EXPLAINED TO US that all we can do on earth is love God.

In order for us not to be indecisive and to know how to do this, Jesus told us that the only way, the only sure recipe, is to love each other.

This love, which is also theological, because it unites us inseparably to Him, is the only door, threshold, and entrance into the very love of God. All paths that are virtues end up at this door.

All of them are really made only to lead us there more rapidly, joyfully, and surely. A virtue that doesn't end up there is a virtue that has gone

---

[7] Madeleine Delbrêl was to write a number of poetic "meditations" in the style of the "Bal de l'Obéissance" ["The Dance of Obedience"] from 1940 to 1950. It was published in the *Vie Spirituelle* [*Spiritual Life*] at the time (cf. *Nous autres, gens des rues* [*We, the Ordinary People of the Streets*], 89). These texts circulated among her close friends, and some of them wanted Madeleine to continue writing and publishing. But she always refused to write what she called "literature." These texts were always written for a specific occasion — a feast or anniversary or a personal note for a variety of circumstances. They remained isolated and sometimes incomplete. In this volume today, we're publishing those we could piece together.

mad. It would circle vainly around God's mountain and fall from the peak of God's love without being able to climb the smooth high walls.

The only vulnerable point and gap is the love of those poor people who are similar to us and not very amiable because they share our own mediocrity.

It could perhaps gratify us to arrive at a sensational level of humility, an unbearable poverty, an imperturbable obedience, or an infallible purity. But if this humility, poverty, purity, and obedience hasn't made us encounter goodness, and if those in our homes, streets, and cities are still as hungry, cold, sad, gloomy, and lonely, we may be heroes, but we aren't among those who love God.

For virtues are like wise virgins who, with their lamps in their hands, remain huddled at this one door — the door of spiritual love and concern for one's brothers and sisters. It's the only door that opens up to God's wedding party with His friends.

Humor in Love[8]

If we're honest with ourselves, it would be really ridiculous not to allow a little humor into our love, for we are rather funny people. But we're not in the mood to laugh at our own buffoonery.

Lord, I love You more than anything . . . in general. But I love this English cigarette, or this Gauloise — in this little minute that's going by — even more than You!

Lord, I give You my life — my whole life . . . but not this little piece of my life — these three minutes . . . when I don't really feel like getting to work.

Lord, for You, I'd conquer this city, France, and the universe. I'd burn myself out for Your Kingdom, but not this little piece of my life, these three minutes, but not to listen to this unbearable creature who tells me her miniscule troubles for the hundredth time!

[8]   1946.

Yes, we're masters of light comedy, and it would be normal that the first audience for this comedy would be ourselves. But that's not the end of the story.

When we've discovered this priceless comic within us, and when we have left with a great burst of laughter while going over the farce of his life, we're tempted to abandon ourselves without delay into a career as a clown for which we, after all, seem rather skilled.

We'd be willingly tempted to think that this isn't very important and that there's room for clowns and puppet characters alongside those who are sublime, strong, and holy. It's certainly not very exciting, but it's not exactly boring either, and that's an advantage.

We must recall that God didn't create us for human loving, but for this enormous and eternal love with which He's loved everything He's created from the outset.

We must accept this love — no longer as God's splendid and magnanimous partner, but as His idiotic beneficiary, who is devoid of charm and basic loyalty.

We're asked to give all we can in this adventure of mercy. We're asked to laugh when this gift fails or is sordid or impure.

But we're also asked to marvel with tears of gratitude and joy at this boundless treasure that flows in us from God's heart.

An unmistakable peace will settle into this intersection of laughter and joy!

Accomplishing on This Earth the Love for Which God Created Us[9]

A Note from 1950

"My little children, love one another" summarizes all that the elderly St. John had to say.

---

[9] Notes written for the intention of her teams.

We love God. The first commandment is the love of God. The second one is like it — that is to say, it's through loving others that we can return the love that God has for us.

The danger is that the second commandment can become the first one. But we have a way of checking this tendency, which is to love everyone, to love Christ, and to love God in each person without any preferences, categories, or exceptions.

The second danger is that we can't and won't be able to do this if we separate love from faith and hope.

Prayer offers faith and hope. We can't love without prayer.

Christ will reveal Himself to us in every person only in prayer through a faith that continues to become more powerful and clear-sighted. We can ask for this gift in prayer, without which there's no love. Our hope will grow through prayer so that we can cope with the number of people we meet and the depth of their needs.

Faith and hope grow through prayer, which will get rid of the obstacle that blocks the path of our love the most: concern for ourselves.

The third danger will be to love not "as Jesus loved us," but in a human way. This is perhaps the biggest danger.

Human love, because it's love, is a great and beautiful thing. Nonbelievers can love each other with a magnificent love. But we haven't been called to this sort of love. It's not *our* love that we have to give. It's the love of God. The love of God is a Divine Person, which is God's gift to us. But it remains a gift which must, so to speak, go through us to go elsewhere — to go toward others.

It's a love that's all-powerful. It doesn't let us put our trust in the power of anything else. It's a gift that can't be kept for ourselves. If we keep it to ourselves, it dies and stops being a gift.

A Note from 1952

The gospel reveals that the love of God is inseparable from the love of people. Loving people isn't a way to love God.

Loving God is a condition in which we can't avoid supernaturally loving people. The means that Christ gave us to help us love God will help us to love others.

The proof of the authenticity of a person's living the gospel in the Church is the intensity of his supernatural love for others. "How can the one who does not love his brother, whom he sees, love God, whom he has not seen?"

So, there can't be any true conflicts between the love of God and the love of neighbor. There can only be false conflicts between them — conflicts in which one of the elements has been incorrectly understood.

Errors in Connection with the Goal

Supernatural love must be Jesus' kind of love — that is, incarnate and redeeming. It's not a spiritual love, but one that's in the flesh (see the parable of the Last Judgment). It's not a love born of the flesh, but born of God. It doesn't offer happiness, but "buys" the Beatitudes. Love becomes an inaccessible goal when we spiritualize it — when we disembody it from its human needs.

Errors in Connection with the Means

The means must be supernatural when the end is supernatural.

Because they concern God, everyone's sins bear something in them that's identical and permanent. The same is true for the suffering that results from them.

Because they are created by people, everyone's sins are both universal and singular. The same is true for the suffering that results from them.

All the means that Christ has given us through His Church and gospel stop being means if we forget the absolute and permanent side of evil. They can also become false ends if we immobilize them and forget the changing and multifarious character of evil.

Christ's redemption — His merciful love — is seen in the healing of the same individual illness in many people occurring one by one in different times, people, and places. It's united and diverse insofar as it restores the plan of God's love in its unity and diversity.

Two Examples of Errors in Our Lives

a) Forms of Prayer

Prayer is the reestablishment of normal relationships between God and ourselves. It's a conversion and turning of our hearts, spirits, and wills toward God, who is always our Creator and Father. Prayer is already love. It asks and it receives. But because we are sinners, it will always be laborious, painful, and disturbing at one time or another. From one perspective, it's already love. From another point of view, it's a sort of necessary and voluntary virtue. That is its permanent aspect.

But the one who has to pray and offer his being to the Spirit's inner "movement" that says "Father" is a person with a particular temperament and particular life circumstances. He was born in a particular era in the midst of a particular group of human beings burdened with particular temptations.

He lives in a big house or an overpopulated room. He works in silence or chaos. He must struggle against solitude or the crowd. His form of morning or evening prayer has to come out of all of this — the prayer of today, the prayer of tomorrow, of his youth, maturity, and old age. Even a Benedictine's prayer of praise, if he wants to leave it in its due place in his life as a means and not make a false end out of it, is modified by his material circumstances.

This means that an evangelical communal life that doesn't include prayer isn't a means of attaining the love of God. But it also means that a communal life that's become satisfied with a fidelity to forms risks turning a means into an end even if the means plays a privileged role in community life.

The protection we provide for prayer must be continually adapted, because prayer is continuously threatened. But the forms that prayer takes must be continually considered as relative and not absolute.

When there seems to be a conflict having to do with the demands of time between fraternal charity and prayer, it's often worthwhile to review the time spent on things that aren't very useful. We must also see if — in order to avoid a precise act of love, which is being asked of us and will cost us a lot — we're not substituting an obligation that is harder and sometimes more painful but preferable to meeting a particular brother. We must finally know that when a vindictive spirit, so rooted in our hearts, has us demand our spiritual "rights," it blinds us from finding the way to fulfill what we need.

Finally, if our love were truly supernatural, it would urge us to pray.

On the other hand, prayer helps us avoid our love becoming disembodied or losing its nature as a supernatural gift.

b) Poverty

Poverty is perhaps more of a means than the other evangelical virtues, because it recognizes that all things are relative means except for love. This is why it can't even be defined, and those who think they have it are actually the ones who lose it.

Poverty is found in and through the mystery of the poor. It resides beyond the detachment from the things to which people give, unjustly, quasi-divine values in the order of efficiency or happiness.

Each epoch doesn't hold onto these things in the same way, nor does each country, race, and environment.

What counts is neither the number of attachments that remain nor what they are, but the number of those we have taken out and our constant effort to continue uprooting them.

The false definitions of poverty — and I think this is very important — often prevent us from being poor. Here's an example:

A century ago, a convent of Poor Clares could own buildings without disturbing any of the nuns.

Our generation became very sensitive to the reality of possessing land or buildings. The fact that you own nothing rather easily gives you a clean conscience.

But now the important and genuine poverty in this matter isn't so much to be or not to be an owner, but to be or not to be housed. We're better off than others in France.

The fact of being housed is a huge privilege on the global scale. If we make this privilege a right, we're richer than a lot of owners.

What I'm saying about housing could be said about the right to work, to live in your own country, and so forth.

There's also a lot to say about the value of power as the contemporary world perceives it.

Some poverty will certainly be required in our time—including the refusal to believe in the Messianism of some milieus or people. Human hope in Jesus' time was undoubtedly linked with the peace of Roman or Greek culture, or perhaps in the suffering mass of slaves, or maybe even in the barbarians who would come to power in the future.

Jesus was neither a Roman citizen, nor a Greek philosopher, slave, or barbarian. He was a member of a small group when it was declining in history—an old great family. He was from Nazareth, "from which nothing good could come."

Christ's poverty is really beyond all poverty. It alone is the mystery of all holy poverty. The role of our poverty is to lead us to participate in it—at the very place where we learn to lose our lives.

A Note from 1956

Missionary teams don't have an earthly kind of love to experience and give as their mission. It's a theological love. It's the love of Jesus Christ, the Son of God, which is only authentic when it includes its human brothers and sisters.

This love motivated by faith leads them to travel the world for the sake of increasing God's glory. They can only contribute to this increase by being an instrument in the development and proclamation of the Faith, for God's glory can only increase through the radiance of the saints, the repentance of sinners, and the enlightenment of nonbelievers.

One single nonbeliever makes God's glory shine if he knows God. This is the basis for our missionary passion.

This love must be purified and expanded in and through communal life. Everything Jesus has said in order for us to love each other can be applied without any restrictions. All the community's members must dedicate themselves to this love.

We owe everything that natural law calls love to our brothers and sisters, so long as we preserve it from oversensitivity, infatuation, and (we'd even be tempted to say) friendships. For the love which is to be experienced is a warm, honest, and devoted brotherly or sisterly love. It's neither sentimental nor passionate, any more than it's icy, rational, or indifferent. But all that natural law requires will be asked of us as well. We are together in order to love the Lord, our only love, more. He wants us to love each other with the love with which He loves us.

In the constant intimacy of our communities, our relationships must be shaped by the discovery of the one to whom we belong as we look for the flourishing of a love among us that Jesus Christ wants.

We can't foresee these relationships. They are caused by what everyone is of himself at each moment.

But the community isn't there for this relationship. Real love is like fire. It doesn't spontaneously stop in front of unburnt fuel. We must be convinced that the fraternal love we owe is an unrestricted and limitless love in any country or milieu. This is the love that proves our faith in God our Father. All people are His children and, consequently, our brothers and sisters.

To refuse this love is to deprive those we know of one of the Gospel's most astonishing revelations, which no mere human has been able to offer to the world.

As far as the actions through which this love is manifested are concerned, we have no right to sort them out in the gospel. We have no right to say that visible help is more of a priority than invisible prayer or sacrifice. One doesn't replace the other. But, in emphasizing the importance of what we don't see, the Lord didn't negate visible help. He was pleased to enumerate examples of it.

Finally, in many cases, the missionary team will connect with local opinions or traditions through certain aspects of its love, while in others it will arouse contempt, mistrust, or mockery. This must not make us want to "keep everything" that Christ wants.

Regarding all these points, communal life must provide support, clarity, and vigilance. This vigilance must be careful not to turn to mistrust or contention. It must give due weight to that which represents the intervention of others in our lives and consider the matter thoroughly when it's about proclaiming the Lord.

To Love to the End

To love "to the end," as the Lord says — this end, which includes martyrdom in so many countries, will, in all likelihood, be more modest for us.

But we must know that the "end" starts when we're in mission territory. Without a natural instinct that helps us or a spontaneous understanding, we must love — if it's really with the love of the Lord that we're loving — not those who are more "related" to us or to an aspect of Christ, but those who are less lovable, those most deprived of goodness and most overwhelmed by evil. This love asks for a complete overturning of ourselves and, if it connects us to the Lord, it puts what seems to be the contradiction of our ability to love in us.

If we make a temporary effort, it's bearable for us. But if we dedicate our whole lives — about which everyone knows what he could have done — we must deal with the revolt of our whole being and trample on it to save it "to the end." That can be very hard.

At this moment, as it was in the beginning, it's up to the missionary team to maintain the Lord's perspective firmly. It's up to the team to alleviate or try to alleviate the pain.

The team must ensure more than ever that it and its members don't instinctively try to find rest from this fierceness in intensified relationships with those we can naturally love. Those who are "less lovable" are often those who love less. This lack of love can become hatred. This hatred doesn't always wound or act, but it can condemn and repel us beyond everyday life. It's especially hard to bear when the "heavy price" to which St. Paul alludes must be paid for the same ones who are driving us away.

At the moment of this breakup — this rejection — we're often so blinded that we can hardly imagine a suffering so harsh; yet this is often the price that must be paid.

For we must know that when we're on a mission, temptations are always adapted to what a determined mission weakens in us or requires of us.

The team can have a very serious role to play if one of its members is being tempted. The Lord doesn't ask us to struggle there by ourselves. He gave us an example by calling on His disciples on the night before His Passion. Many of His friends had abandoned Him when He asked the Father why He was being abandoned. For those of us who are not Christ, the pretense of abandonment normally results in despair. In those circumstances, a brotherly love that doesn't uphold its responsibilities would be a seriously inadequate form of love.

We don't "make" love, even if it's ours. God and God alone can "make" love. We have to ask Him for it and receive it. Like poor signposts, we have to lay down the acts of authentic human love that God asks us for and that make us deserving of it. We are not to be agitators in our charitable works. We have to be passive and patient and let

God's suffering, patient love work in us. It's through *that* and only through that that God's loving action can reach the world.

A Spirituality of the Bike[10]

"Go," you tell us at all the Gospel's turning points. To be headed in your direction, we must go, even when our laziness begs us to stay put.

You have chosen a strange balance for us. It's a balance that can only be established and kept if we're moving.

This is a little like a bike that doesn't hold up without moving — a bike that keeps leaning against a wall as long as we haven't gotten on it to make it move along the road.

The condition that's given to us is a universal and dizzying insecurity. Our life tilts and gives out as soon as we take a look at it.

We can only stand by walking and getting a move on in a momentum of love.

All or many of the saints who have been given to us as models had an insurance plan — a kind of spiritual security that guaranteed against risks and illness and that even took care of their spiritual creations. They had official prayer times, ways of doing penance, and a whole code of advice and defense.

But the adventure of Your grace is made available to us in quite a vulnerable state. You refuse to provide us with a road map. Our journey happens at night. Each act that's to be done in turn is illuminated like signal relays. Often, the only guarantee is this regular weariness of having the same work to do every day, the same housework to take up again, the same faults to correct, and the same mistakes not to make.

But outside of this guarantee, everything else is up to Your imagination, which is at ease with us.

---

[10] Written around 1945 – 1950.

Long Live Freedom[11]

One is a Christian by and through love — by nothing else and for nothing else.

If you forget love, you make yourself absurd. If you betray it, you become monstrous. No justice can avoid its law. If you turn from it to receive something greater than it, you're preferring wealth to life. If you turn away from it to give something better than it, you deprive the whole world of the only treasure you were made to give. If love is practically optional for you, you should not have bothered with Abidjan or someplace else, for you're only good for nothing. We're free of any obligation, but totally dependent on only one need: love.

Love is more than what's needed to exist, experience, and act. Love is our life becoming eternal. When we leave love behind, we leave our lives behind. An action without love is a sudden death. A loving act is an immediate resurrection. You can't fabricate love. You receive it. Incomplete love is a gift that's incompletely received. Perfect love is a gift that's completely received. Love is free just as much as it's needed. You don't win it in a contest. You win it by wanting it, asking for it, receiving it, and transmitting it. We don't learn about love. We get to know it gradually by getting to know Christ.

Christ's faith makes us capable of being loving. Christ's life reveals love to us. Christ's life shows us how to desire, ask for, and receive love. Christ's spirit makes us alive with love, act with love, and fruitful with love.

Everything can be used for love. Without it, everything is barren — ourselves first and foremost.

---

[11] Written for a team that was going to the Ivory Coast, 1961.

To Become Poor

The Poverty of the One Who Is on the Move[12]

THE ONE WHOSE SPIRIT is connected to you must remain in motion. We always imagine that in order to travel, we need roads, landmarks, and different countries. So, your way isn't that. It's simply life. It's a life that flows, in which we keep going even if we've cast our moorings.

One day, I met a man on one of our suburban streets. It wasn't heroic. I would have gladly thought he was a passing angel. He was, in reality, only a poor lodger in the home. But this man who I saw go by explained to me — better than a lot of books had done — and showed me what true poverty is for the one who is on the move — traveling light without possessions — in Your Spirit.

He had very ordinary clothes that we didn't notice. He looked straight ahead of him with an illuminating clarity. The whole street was rejuvenated and seemed to exist for the first time.

He wasn't carrying anything in his hands. His pockets were flat and seemed light. Both his hands were open and floated in the air around him.

[12]   Meditation, 1946 – 1948.

Maybe he was a little crazy. Yet he was a lesson in wisdom. All his work seemed to go through things and people. He was like a parable — like a sign of true poverty. "For if you love only those who love you," you won't need to keep going. They will come to you. But if you love those who don't love you, you'll need to walk at all times to meet them.

This is the poverty of the one who is on the move.

The number of things that prevent us from being agile and light is amazing. We're not aware of it, but if, from one day to the next, we lost everything, we'd close to a whole lot of people who seem to us to be living at the end of the world.

"I understood through St. Thomas, sir, that, after all, God may be credible. But who is telling me, that for you, St. Thomas was the most boring and incomprehensible teacher?"

"My religion, sir, is inseparable from this very wise morality that produced this beautiful family I belong to."

"But who is telling me that your family wasn't produced at all, and if you want to love Jesus Christ, after all, nothing in the world could ever make you love morality?"

"The Church, for me, sir, is inseparable from this healthy approach."

"But who is telling me that your heart is irresistibly inclined toward anarchy?"

Whoever wants to meet his brothers and sisters needs a royal indifference for all that isn't this naked, basic faith that makes him lose his memory, tastes, and originality. This is a faith that makes us ordinary with this great banality that saints have accepted. It led them to the end of the earth.

For the price of poverty is an exorbitant cost. It's bought from the sacrifice of everything that's not the Kingdom of God.

We'll be interested in everything that interests others, virtuous through a heroism that didn't attract us, and become the brothers of people who were never like us.

Those who will meet us on their way will stretch out their eager hands for a treasure that will spring from us. It will be a treasure that will be freed from our earthen vessels, colorful baskets, trunks, and baggage. It will be a simply divine treasure that will be fashionable for everyone because it will stop being dressed in our fashion.

So, we will be agile and, in turn, become parables — the parable of the single, miniscule, round, and precious pearl for which we've sold everything.

Poverty and the Poor

A Note from 1956

Wealth isn't always a question of material goods that we own, or even of culture, education, and so on.

To be rich is to be powerful.

Even God's gifts are riches. Yes, "sell everything that you have." But if you have nothing to sell, take a good look at what you have. We can't make ourselves poor. I think that we have more to offer than we realize. But, even more, we have to be patient and to give, sell, prune, suppress, and start over, while still knowing our inability to wholly give up what power we do have.

For real poverty is the desert that flourishes again, the new life that comes out of solitude, the obedience in which my will bends but remains what it was, and the poverty that never finishes eliminating the rich man that we are. We can sketch it in us like children's drawings. But only God offers it.

He alone can give the celibate the spirit of solitude because of the Kingdom of Heaven. He alone can make an obedient person out of a resigned person. He alone can make a poor person out of someone who is simply impoverished.

A Note from 1964

The poor aren't only brothers and sisters to love in a brotherly way *because* they are brothers and sisters. They are also "our lords the poor" *because* the poor person is our Lord. The poor person is the sacrament of our encounter with Christ and of our love that is given to Christ. There's nothing platonic about the parable of the Last Judgment.

Thus, whatever form poverty takes in our lives, we can't be faithful to Jesus Himself if the poor can't enter our life circumstances *as if they were at home* — just as Christ is at home with us — if they aren't a *priority*. (There are multiple forms of priority. But they are always particular.)

We can hold forth on Christ's poverty — on His imitation and how He calls us to live it out.

It's indisputable that, whatever our life is, in order for it to be Christian, our relationship to the poor must be similar to the way Jesus would welcome them and relate to them.

The poor, because of their very poverty, are often repulsive (kissing the leper). They bring Christ's contradiction into our lives.

Christ's real presence in the one who is poor and known as a real person is perhaps — when it's really believed — what can shatter any social situation and make it authentically Christian.

The poor person must not be someone who is merely *tolerated*; he must be *expected*. We must not have him undergo some kind of test. "We'll do this up to here, that up to there." He never owes us anything. We owe him what we owe Christ Himself.

This is the same faith that lets us receive Christ through the Eucharist into ourselves and through the poor person into our lives.

Who is my neighbor? Anybody.

Who is the poor person? Generally, anyone who is "outside" — outside other people's lives. He's a prisoner, a sick person, a stranger, naked, and so forth.

Our Solitude

Wherever We Are[13]

SOLITUDE, MY GOD, ISN'T simply being alone. You are there, in our solitude, because everything that's apart from You either passes away or joins You.

What good would it do us to go to the end of the earth to find a desert? What good would it do us to enter walls that would separate us from the world, because You wouldn't be *there* any more than You would be in the clamor of machines or a crowd of eight hundred faces?

Are we childish enough to think that all these people who are gathered together are big, important, and alive enough to block our horizon when we look to You?

Being alone isn't having gone beyond people or having left them behind. Being alone means knowing You are great, my God — that You alone are great and that there's little difference between the immensity of grains of sand and the immensity of human lives that are gathered together.

---

[13] Meditation written between 1945 and 1946.

The difference doesn't damage solitude, for what makes these human lives more present and visible to the eyes of our souls is this communication they have with You. It's this prodigious resemblance to the only one who is. It's like a part of You, and this glimpse doesn't wound our solitude.

To know once in your lifetime that you're alone! To have once met — perhaps in a true desert — the bush that burned without destroying itself — the bush of the one who established solitude in us forever.

When Moses once encountered the inexpressible bush, he was able to return to people while carrying a permanent desert in himself. So, let's not blame the world or life for veiling Christ's face for us. Let's find this face. It will veil and absorb everything.

Let's leave our childishness behind.

The wood that burns in the fire doesn't care about the landscape. We live in a tremendous blaze. If it doesn't burn us, it's because our feet are nearby. It's not the scenery's fault.

This Is How We Discover Our Souls[14]

It takes such a long time, Lord, to understand that we can be loved only with mercy, and that no esteem, admiration, or trust can come to us from You without having passed through Your mercy.

It takes a long time, but it comes. Thus, like a blind and deaf child on its mother's lap, who is submerged in darkness and solitude, we'll one day discover that our soul is completely unable to see the eternal hills and hear Your echoes in Paradise. So, we discover our souls on the lap of Your Providence.

Your Spirit surrounds us — this finger of the Father's right hand — like the hand of a mother that reveals, teaches, and brings her child back to life.

[14] 1946.

With a push, Your Spirit guides us. With a touch, He announces Himself. His soundless embrace sows our hearts with the seed of Your words.

The silence of Your Spirit responds to the words we say in our silence and darkness — a silence whose nearness surrounds us and teaches us.

For this to occur, it's enough to know that our eyes can't see and our ears can't hear everything that You are.

Our Deserts[15]

When we love each other, we love to be together, and when we're together, we love to talk to each other. When we love each other, it's annoying to have a lot of people around us. When we love each other, we love to listen to the other person alone, without other voices that might intrude or interrupt.

This is why those who love God have always cherished the desert and why God can't refuse it to those who love Him.

I'm sure, Lord, that You love me and that this desert where we encounter You can't be unavailable even in this life, so cluttered and affected from every direction by family, friends, and everyone else.

We never go to the desert without crossing a lot of difficulties, without being tired from a long journey, and without tearing out our eyes from the monotonous horizon.

Deserts are won, not given. We only tear away the deserts in our lives from the mystery of our human hours by disrupting our habits and laziness. It's hard, but essential to our love. Long hours of drowsiness aren't worth ten minutes of real sleep. The solitude we spend with You is like this.

Hours of almost being solitary are less restful than a moment of being immersed in Your presence.

[15] Written between 1945 and 1950.

This isn't about learning how to waste time. We must learn to be alone each time life reserves a break for us. Life is full of breaks that we can discover or waste. How amazing to foresee all these face-to-face meetings on the heaviest and bleakest of days.

What a joy it is to know that we'll be able to look up to Your face while the porridge is thickening, while the phone keeps ringing, while we wait at the stop sign for the bus that isn't coming, while we're climbing the stairs, or while we're going to dig around in the garden for some pieces of parsley to finish the salad.

What an extraordinary walk we'll have coming back from the subway tonight when we'll no longer be able to see clearly the people we meet on the sidewalk.

How advantageous these delays will be when we're waiting for a spouse, friends, or children.

All of the hurrying about that isn't happening is often the sign of a desert. But our deserts have some rough defenses — even if only our impatience, wandering thoughts, or drowsiness when we're on the lookout for a vacation.

For we're fashioned such that we can't prioritize You without a pathetic struggle. You, our Beloved, will always be weighed against this fascination and exhausting obsession with our trifles.

Notes on Solitude[16]

Solitude and Celibacy

Even if the collective belongs to God and exists only for Him, each one of us belongs to Jesus Christ alone, our God and Lord, in a unique way.

This means that if we haven't been called to solitude, we won't have found our niche here.

There are many ways of understanding the evangelical counsels and teachings of Christ without disagreeing with the Church.

---

[16] Notes written for the intention of her teams, 1956.

There are different kinds of poverty, celibacy, and obedience that don't require solitude. We can, for example, choose celibacy so to be more available to our neighbor while making this celibacy a gift from God.

On the contrary, a contemplative religious chooses celibacy because of God, and she knows that her visible and tangible neighbor plays a less important role in her choice.

There's a risk of uncertainty for us.

If we choose celibacy, it's to belong to the Lord, and by Him, because of Him, and in Him, to those we love as He loves us and that we must love as ourselves.

Two errors await us here and, at some point, they will surprise us if they aren't detected.

Having chosen the Lord, we won't understand why He's chosen so many neighbors for us. Or, having accepted ahead of time the neighbor He promised us, we'll be surprised that at other times the earth has been emptied for us, so to speak.

So, the Lord doesn't give us any guarantee about either hypothesis. Thus, we have to be ready for both. What I'm saying about celibacy could also be said about all the great evangelical demands when they are accepted or chosen for Christ, or chosen for one of the tasks He has designated.

The risk of doubt increases for us because we're expecting a different solitude than the one we're getting, and are unaware to what extent a simple event can make our neighbors seem to us like hostile strangers.

The solitude that we're talking about here will never be spared for us. If it were, it would be a great misfortune, for it is inseparable from our belonging to the Lord. Not to have known this solitude in our lives would be a sign that our relationship to God was ruptured.

We'll rediscover it in ourselves, first of all. An average celibate generally drags the phantom of the wife he never had with him all his life. His "complement" follows him like a worn shadow. This shadow is anonymous for some people. For others, it has a series of faces.

We must be aware of this solitude. It's healthy as long as it's voluntarily taken on and fully identified and joyfully worn on that day by a free person. He's happy to choose the one he prefers, even if it makes him suffer. Despite that, we must know that on some days, it will still be fearsome and cruelly burdensome. This will occur when we have a great joy or a great weariness to share.

Accepting and choosing to prioritize a few minutes of this solitude will be the most authentic moment we can offer to God when we die.

Solitude and the Apostolate

But solitude won't only come to us. In a way, the more apostolic a life becomes, the more solitary it becomes.

Apostolic love actually entails knowing people in the way we know people we love, and this is done through creating connections. Those sinners, indifferent people, nonbelievers, and atheists that we love in this way are neighbors who are close to us. But everything that makes them our neighbors "apostolically" makes them different from us and creates areas of solitude between them and us.

This solitude will be especially more difficult to bear and will seem more abnormal as it imposes itself in the midst of more intimate relationships and warmer friendships. It could at that moment become a dangerous temptation or an atmosphere that's suitable for temptations if we haven't been careful about it.

We must approach solitude positively—the one we're talking about here as well as the one we'll look for in some "desert." For if some people are looking for certain deserts, it's good that they know that solitude that is imposed, which they find in themselves, is something good.

That solitude is something good is a truth that takes a long time to learn. That solitude is inevitable for man is a truth that's quicker to learn. It's still quicker to learn for a Christian.

Man always stumbles — even with the person he loves the most — upon an inevitable solitude that encloses something of him within himself. The Christian, through that very part of himself which separates him from unbelievers, stumbles upon that which, in God, reveals itself to his reason without requiring faith. It is then that everything becomes apparent to him, which, for man left to himself, turns God into a stranger.

It's this first glimpse of solitude that the Christian must recognize at once as the true place of his encounter with the Lord.

We still have to make a special place where God comes to join us in this solitude which increases with the conditions of life that are brought to it.

Much human sadness is solitude. If we honor God by being joyful, all our solitudes will be inhabited by Him.

Solitude and Community Life

Community life must help us keep, find, and love solitude. If we don't stress the means that it gives us ahead of time, we risk not recognizing them when we face them. On the subject of unity and the desire to achieve it, there are many anxieties. If they are translated, they are signs of solitude for us — types of identifiers.

We wouldn't be women if on some days we didn't suffer bitterly from not being understood either by someone or, who knows, even by everyone.

There's something in everyone that will never be understood by anyone. That something is the very cause of our solitude, which is intrinsic to us. We must, first of all, accept this basic solitude.

There are various ways of not accepting it. Some withdraw into themselves and are silent. But it's not a good silence. This is the classic attitude of the woman who isn't understood. Others, on the contrary, relentlessly explain themselves or, more often, make people understand the most minute nuances of their way of thinking.

In either case, they get stuck in their frustration — either silently or verbally — which gives the impression of a disagreement. In reality, it's only one of our notes that no human ear can hear.

The day we understand that this incurable rift between others and ourselves is the place where God calls us by name — through all the loves and influences we've experienced, the trials we've endured, and the selves that we are — we'll have undergone a great reversal that turns a grave solitude into a blessed solitude.

Solitude and the Love of God[17]

Love knows it's stronger than anything. It loves to struggle. When love is fighting, it mocks itself while nevertheless seeing the greatest obstacles between itself and the world topple. Each obstacle measures its strength, while love humbles itself all the more by remaining true to itself.

We must not forget all that when we're talking about love — the love of God.

Without solitude, we would perhaps never know if we've tried to love God or if we've been merely living a romantic or intellectual fantasy.

But we must recognize our solitude — the one we don't go looking for, the one God carries to where we are.

If we don't recognize it, we risk being misled by it without knowing it or missing the meeting with God that it always entails.

Even if we recognize it, we have to pay attention. Solitude is contradictory. It's penitent but loving. Even if we accept its severity, we'll often fail to stop there. Its severity is only transitory. We wait while pacing back and forth. But God won't stop coming as long as we don't stop waiting for Him.

Later — where it's light — we'll be awed by how brief our solitudes were. I say brief because these long solitudes are made up of very small solitudes that follow each other like pearls. We wear ourselves out because we don't know how to itemize them.

[17] Excerpt from a letter, 1954.

Silence[18]

SILENCE HAS AN IMPORTANT role in religious life. Many people who aren't necessarily religious practice and need silence for their research, work, and projects. Silence is doomed to a limited space for the Christian who lives a secular life. It's used as an aid to prayer and is its prerequisite when this prayer takes on the exceptional form of a retreat.

We're generally sure that we're encountering silence in our search for God before believing that we're encountering God.

Two expressions can be used for silence — being silent and creating silence.

Being silent can mean that we've arrived. Creating silence means that we're working on it.

But the perspective of secular life on this point is that, contrary to what happens in religious life, we try to use silence, but *we can't use silence* for people and things that surround us without sharing our lives.

If we wait for silence in order to pray, we run the risk of rarely praying. Or if we pray, it won't be in the parts of the world that lack prayer the most: big cities, where work and amusement join forces against silence.

---

[18] Notes written for her teams, 1956.

Even if this seems paradoxical, it's by giving silence the role it plays in the most religious of religious lives that we'll be able to put it into our lives, because we'll prioritize it over all else. If silence is necessary to find God, we can be sure that God gives it to us. We're the ones who don't know how to find it.

Silence doesn't exist in order for us to be quiet. In this case, it would resemble being mute, which has never been anything other than an infirmity among beings whom God has blessed with the gift of speech — in order to talk, presumably.

Creating silence is listening to God! It's suppressing everything that prevents us from listening to or hearing God. Using silence is listening to God wherever He's speaking — from those to whom He speaks in the Church to those Christ identified with in another way and who ask us for light, our hearts, or bread.

It's listening to God wherever He expresses His will in prayer and other situations that aren't prayer in the strict sense of the word.

We need silence to do God's will — silence that's sustained through this other practice, which we tend to cut out of our lives a lot or ignorantly scorn — *meditation*. We must meditate on the impressions, hints, invitations, and orders of God's will, just as the farmer gathers his harvest in the barn or the scientist reaps the fruit of his experiment. Gathering our thoughts or meditating is never done without silence. They are never done without movement. The peasant will store or sell his harvest, and the scientist will confirm the findings of his experiment through replication.

Because the Word was made flesh, we can't know Him without listening to Him. But we know Him even less when we don't try to love Him as we listen, when we don't try to imitate Him in the flesh while we're living His life, and when we fail to follow His Word where it wants to lead us. It wants to lead us into the depths of the covenant between God and ourselves — to the possibility of uniting our will to His and to the possibility that our acts would become His.

We don't experience the mystery of this covenant — of which all love on earth is only an image — if we bear less silence and less meditation — only to pile up a new kind of fruit or get in touch with a little more of the secret of the world.

It seems to me to be impossible to envision an evangelical life without wanting a life of silence and knowing what that entails.

If we note from one end of the Gospel to the other what Jesus said about the Word of God — all that He says about it being "received," "listened to," "kept," "done," and "announced" — we'll soon know for sure that the good news needs to be welcomed, received, and carried into the deepest part of ourselves in order to be known, experienced, and communicated.

If our whole life must be subject to the gospel of Jesus Christ and if we're willing to take all of His Word as a guide in the course of life's circumstances, it will be impossible for our life not to be silent.

Today, in our own circumstances, and in the countries where we currently are, we must find out what silence is required of us and what "superstitions" prevent us from achieving it.

It goes without saying that a rowdy person, a braggart, a great talker, or an abuser are opposed to silence. But we're much less convinced that a ruckus, brass bands, glasses, houses, and cities are obstacles to silence.

The rowdy person, the braggart, and the abuser go further than merely not listening to the Lord: they interrupt Him. Even more, they contradict Him. For the rowdy person is the one who attracts attention to himself even when he's at the end of the line. He makes noise for fear of being forgotten. The braggart is the one who needs an orchestra in order to act. He's his own orchestra before, during, and after what he does. Whether they like it or not, his neighbors have to be his audience. The great talker may never have had the opportunity to give an eloquent speech, but he considers each of his phrases to be as important as a speech. The great talker gets so much pleasure in conversing with his fellows that he endlessly speaks about his problems but isn't interested in a solution. The abuser can't be someplace without breaking something. Moreover, he specializes in very diverse things. He's the one who has every good reason to be irritated and who damages all the objects he uses. But he's also the one whose words only know how to hurt people's feelings, reputations, hopes, and hearts.

Few of us never fill any of these roles. Even if our cramped living conditions force us not only to hear all the words that a crowded family can say in a day, but also our neighbors' conversations coming through our thin walls, we must be really convinced that these are *words* that we pronounce, words that are contrary to the gospel and destroy silence, first and foremost.

If we blame the noise people make, we also ordinarily blame the noise things make. The first question we could ask ourselves is if we're accusing this noise of preventing our relationship with God or only the normal activities of our lives.

Here's another similar question. Noise doesn't prevent many people from working, but it's constantly tiring, whether we're aware of it or not. Hence, there's often an unexpected feeling of well-being when we move away from where we live and the noise that occurs there. Having experienced the satisfaction of comfortably praying to God, having peacefully reflected on His business and our own, and having enjoyed a completely natural rest, we can have trouble adjusting to a Christian life as experienced by the Christians tired of noise that we are.

Finally, let's repeat what we said about actual prayer, if the noise and lack of space that increase in a home — like machines that increase the intense noise in some workshops — excludes silence, and if some silence is needed to hear and experience the Gospel of Jesus Christ, we'd have to conclude that the poor can't be evangelized, which is contrary to what the Lord offered as proof of His mission.

It seems that a basic silence for us could be described in a secular sounding phrase: "We don't interrupt God." There are people we can listen to who speak to God for hours without appearing to cut Him off. They seem to be like a long-lasting uninterrupted echo of His Word — an echo that's more or less complete — admittedly weak, yet still an echo.

Others, on the contrary, seem, in some circumstances — while keeping quiet — to interrupt God and prevent Him from transmitting words through them that they could have echoed.

But it is not only the human aspect of our words that interests silence, but also that of the Word of God, the Word of God made flesh, so that the Word of God can be proclaimed through everything that makes a man human, so that it may be inscribed even in his flesh. Our entire life must create silence and silence everything in us that speaks selfishly and arrogantly. Our whole life must silence everything that's come into us from outside — every opinion that is without God's influence, everything that makes real noise and is an obstacle to God's Word.

We have to be in direct contact with Christ's words, actions, examples, and teachings. They must not be stifled, muffled, or minimized by the dust of our thoughts, desires, or self-centeredness.

We must not interrupt God.

This effort is humbly accessible to us because it's asked of us. Everything that's capable of loving in us leads to our loving God. Nothing is declared to be lowly.

So, if a mother doesn't love her child any less in a motel than in a room in her home; if two engaged people judge the value of a crowd — even if it's a game or meeting — by whether or not they will be there together; if two lovers are able to talk quietly in an uproar, whereas the unrequited lover is told "I didn't hear what you said, I was thinking of something else," we can hope that our love of God will help create this silence in our lives. If this part of us remains indifferent, we can at least compare our love for God with the love of the human heart for what it loves.

For if a mother loves her child at home or on the road, her love costs her more on the road than at home. It costs her more in a shabbily furnished room than in a decent home. If the members of a household can love each other a lot in an abnormally overcrowded building, they love each other with a love that's more costly than in the idyllic "nest" of a young family.

Love comes at a high cost in all miseries — the miseries of budgets, of bodies and nerves — so that everyone, rich or poor, can keep what remains silent within himself because it already belongs to what the other desires.

This silence that makes those who love each other compatible, the solitude that's impossible to suppress in each one of us, these are the two bulwarks against everything which threatens love.

How could our love for God cost less?

In this silence in which the difficulties to overcome are so great that we instinctively ask God for help, it's perhaps good to start modestly with what's closest to us, but to ask God to help us as well.

Given that some of our words can be contrary to the Gospel, I don't think we can seriously look for silence without doggedly and clearly working to remove our habit of useless words. Nothing other than their suppression would give our lives new lungs to breathe with. In the past, we said that women "gossiped." If gossiping is a feminine predisposition, it would be less harmful — if we cannot suppress it all at once — to use it to "gossip with God." It would perhaps not be much worse than being conceited enough to let Him know about grandiose things.

Later, we could perhaps use this time to let the Lord talk to us clearly or indirectly.

On the contrary, what is told to us must never seem useless to us. It's marvelous to be able to communicate with others through words.

If a subject of conversation isn't interesting to us, the one who is speaking is. Real charity must always go before silence.

But when we have the opportunity to be really silent, we must not pass it up. If we don't have pauses of real silence, we very quickly no longer know what it is. A half hour of total silence gives us a better explanation of silence than many hours that are riddled with words. We need these lessons because collective silence is disappearing more and more. Citing the radio, the theater, horns, and heavy traffic isn't new.

In order to intersperse our days with silence, we could begin observing silence when we might otherwise indulge in obsessive thinking. This would be a really very modest manifestation of a phenomenon which, alas, doesn't seem very amazing to us. With Christ, we are going to do what we have to do together.

It's rather certain that in retrieving the time that's given to useless conversations — the asides that diverge from our originally purposeful conversations — we will find something to welcome, keep, and transmit the Gospel word.

Yet, we'll still need to prove that we love the one who speaks this word to us. This will happen when we can speak only to Him and are silent only with Him. For there are circumstances when we're forced to be silent. There can be many different kinds of them, and they can often surprise us. We must then become their disciples and learn to endure — often as a kind of suffering — what we had looked for and cherished as a blessing.

Humble and Gentle Hearts

The Unprivileged[19]

ONLY GENTLE AND HUMBLE hearts can experience Christ's law. Gentleness and humility are Jesus Christ's very features — in His filial love for God and His fraternal love for people.

Regardless of their personal gifts, their place in society, their jobs, possessions, class, or race, and regardless of the development of power and human science or the tremendous discoveries of humanity and its history, Christians continue to be little people — *little people.*

They are little before God because they were created by Him and are dependent on Him.

Regardless of the directions their lives have taken and the things they have accumulated along the way, they came from God and are going back to Him.

They are gentle, like weak and loving children who are close to their strong and loving Father.

[19]   1962.

They are little because they know they are with God, don't know much, aren't capable of much, and are limited in their knowledge and love.

They don't talk about God's will in the events that are occurring or about what Christ has commanded them to do. For their part, they carry God's will out themselves in these events.

They are gentle like the confident and active performers of a work whose enormity escapes them but in which they recognize their task.

They are little when they are with people. They are little, unimportant people, not great historical figures. They have no privileges, rights, or possessions, are superior to no one. They are gentle because they are tenderly respectful of God's creation, wounded and marred by violence. They are gentle because they themselves are victims of evil and are contaminated by it.

They all have the vocation of being pardoned — not innocent.

Christians are dedicated to struggle. They don't have any privileges, but their mission is to triumph over evil. They don't have any rights, but they have the duty to fight misfortune, which is the consequence of evil.

There's only one weapon for this, and that's their faith. It's a faith they must proclaim, a faith that transforms evil into good if they themselves accept suffering as a path to salvation for the world — if they think that dying is offering their lives, and if everyone's pain becomes their own.

They work like Christ and with and through Christ in time by their words, actions, suffering, and death.

Humility[20]

If community life helped us become more humble, it would be such a precious thing that we could hardly imagine it. But such a life more

---

[20]   Notes written for the intention of her teams, 1956.

modestly has to help us know first that we are arrogant from the moment of our entering the world. Then, it must help us become, or at least try to become, little people in the little world.

After we've come to the end of this initial work, this life could perhaps give us work that's harder and less discernible when it's offered to us. It could perhaps help us not reject the beginnings of real humility as a curse. Only God can give these to us. They are mostly hidden in humiliations but are among his most beautiful gifts.

Community Life Must Help Us Know That We're Arrogant

Confessing the damage we've caused one of our brothers or sisters is indispensable, but if we believe the Church thinks this is enough, we're badly mistaken. The Church wants the evil we've done to be repaired as much as possible.

But because a certain sin can't be directly repaired, in that case, we do what we can to repair it in prayer or by burdensome acts of another kind. This doesn't mean that in this way we can directly repair what is repairable at the level where the wrong was committed.

For example, if we've harmed a work companion at his job, and if he is burdened by the consequences of our sin in his work, we could overwhelm him with proof of our devotion — even on a practical level. We could fail to do what we should do — *repair* the damage to his work that we're responsible for.

However, if we happen to accept criticisms that seem really unfair, it's extremely rare for us to indicate the damage we could have caused without being invited to do so. I've often noticed that in the exceptional cases in which we declare ourselves to be responsible, we don't do it in front of the people we have hurt. Our acts of reparation are very rare.

Let's not delude ourselves. Our collective exclamations about our common misery hardly replace a clear and precise acknowledgement of our personal sins. It's honest to be aware of this attitude. It's a trick we have to teach ourselves. Here's a way we can do this. The other ways risk doing more harm than good. We should focus on refusing to let our sins be anonymous. We must not accept this anonymity more than we'd accept an accusation coming from someone who isn't guilty. When we do this, we're affirming that being in the light or vegetating in the darkness are conditions of life and death. We're giving everyone a share in his love for clarity, so that a climate can be created where each person will go against the flow of his arrogance.

Community Life Must Help Us Become Little People

This is the essence of what we learn in community.

Whatever our gift to God is, it will never be but a gift that God made for us and that we're giving back to Him. God will always be "the one who loved us first." Loving Him will always involve receiving His love, first of all.

But one thing we don't always know is that in order to receive God's blessings, we must learn to receive gifts from people.

We can be disoriented by a false notion of fraternal charity and thus lose a part of our "ability" to receive God. God will always give Himself to *little people*, and we must perceive the lack of logic there is in our only wanting to be the *great one* who gives while continuing to be the *little one* who receives from God.

The Gospel parables aren't poetry. The last ones who will be first aren't the last ones from our imaginations — not even our kinds of last people who give and give of themselves. They are the last ones that people consider to be the last ones without asking for their opinion. They are people who must ask everyone for everything because they have nothing that allows them to have something. They are people who receive the characteristic of being last from others.

This quality can't be created. God allows it for the person He wants to have it. We are to respect what resembles it in our lives.

It's sometimes useful to look at the gifts others have given. It's always good to be grateful. It's also good to indicate what we want to do alone and at all costs, and what we really need and don't ask for simply because we don't want to ask for it. It's particularly useful to do it when we normally wouldn't have to ask for anything. We're often in such a hurry.

It's good to recognize all this help as coming from God *through* others. There's a gap between a favor we ask for in the simplest way possible — but with the conviction that it's owed to us — and the favor we ask for like the poor person we always are — though we're often unaware of it — like a "poor person who isn't entitled to anything."

It's necessary to strive with all one's strength to be the one who is devoted, makes sacrifices, and spares no expense for others. But if we want to be self-sufficient in everyday life as well as in the pains and difficulties of a Christian life, something in us will remain dangerously great.

Being a "good example" for others is surely a necessary task since its opposite is scandal. However, this good example will never be completely good if we haven't first discovered it and then tried to follow the good example that another person had to give us, that everyone had to give us, if we want to be someone else's disciple for this or that.

While still on the question of the example, we must really know that we don't always provide a good example. Even in moments when we struggle most firmly against ourselves, we remain indebted to the example that we should give. For us to be consoled, we must know that a good example is always available to us — the example of one who thinks it's normal to rebuke him at times for faults that he actually recognizes before God.

The day we are convinced that we're little people — a small world community — and treat each other like this — without being astonished at who we are — many things in our lives will minimally but truly harmonize with God's simplicity.

Community Life Can Help Us, but It Can Also Harm Us

It's very striking that regardless of the community they belong to, people — without any pangs of conscience — transfer the faults, actions, and vices to it that that same conscience forbids them to do in their personal lives.

Thus, we often see communities made up of brave people acting greedily, hypocritically, and disloyally. Each of these brave people thought they were doing their duty because it was for "the good" of this or that thing.

It would be too optimistic to think that our group escapes this law completely. It, at least, retains the ability to tempt us, and if we're not aware of this kind of temptation, it turns something good into something evil. However, we have a way to cut out everything that, in sum, we'd consider to be a perversion of the group — everything that would lead us to turn away from our goal — even through a single action. We can refuse to accept the group as an entity *in itself*. We must be convinced that the group doesn't exist in itself.

On the one hand, it exists only in relation to God. On the other hand, it exists in relation to each one of us, and not an *us* that would be something other than the sum of what each individual is personally.

The "good of the group" is that it helps everyone to belong to God. This good can't, in any case, justify actions that God wouldn't want us to commit in each of our lives. There isn't a good "for the group" in the world that can transform a lack of charity into an act of charity, pride into humility, something untrue into something true, or small betrayals into loyalty, merely because it's done in the group's favor.

God doesn't let His children perform these actions whether they are done in a group or alone.

Don't Humiliate Anyone

We can't receive humility from God if we haven't done everything possible to avoid humiliating ourselves or our neighbor. It's much easier than we may think to humiliate someone — often even without his knowing it or our finding it to be unusual.

Humiliating someone is treating him as less than ourselves. It's respecting him less than we respect ourselves — even if he's absent.

I think that to humiliate someone is almost always not only to be sure that he's less valuable than us, but that this gives us the right to indisputable privileges.

For it would be naïve to think that when we become aware of what we call the social injustices — and not some social injustices — we'd have reached the end of the list of privileges for some and disadvantages for others.

The social injustices that have been the most spotlighted in our time — even for those of us who are the most aware — have aspects or consequences that we don't discern — just as we don't discern things which are too close to us without getting far enough away from them.

We're even more like near-sighted people without glasses about countless injustices, which are always accompanied by their corresponding privileges that people living in society modify and sometimes turn upside down. But they always let just as many exist — even if that means producing new ones.

Let me take a very simple example. I don't know if there's a single society that has instinctively or very scientifically made people citizens of well-determined categories of happiness. The powerful of any kind are determined to delight the happy poor person and the unhappy poor person. This applies to all levels of society.

At the same time, the same justice is used there. The "righteous person," who is well adjusted to his society, works to lead people he meets to a happy frame of mind that corresponds to their areas of influence. And they are the righteous ones!

This is how — we're starting to say it a lot — the rich judge the poor, but also how the intelligent judge those who are considered to be unintelligent, the able-bodied judge the disabled, the healthy judge the sick, those who are in relationships judge those who are isolated, the son of a family judges the man without a family, and so forth. We could go on indefinitely while being sure of touching upon a subject that we really don't know about.

What we call "poverty," whether it's chosen or accepted, only consists of acts of goodwill that express our desire to God to be really poor through the poverty that only He can give us. It gets confused with humility, which alone makes us what we are in truth: little people.

To humiliate someone is to treat him like somebody over whom we have power. It's as easy to do this as to treat him as less than ourselves.

Society — as we know it — teaches us mutual tyranny just as it teaches us false justice.

The dependencies of one person upon another are called social relationships. Many of them would be neither good nor bad if the spirit that flows in them wasn't a spirit of power.

We draw a box around our acts of obedience, so to speak, and we drink our acts of oppression like water. We unconsciously make people subject to them. Some of these acts invade our whole lives like fine dust.

Here's another simple example. Let's take the sort of tacit agreement in a brotherhood like ours — and we'll find the same thing in many families, professions, and such like. The conventional "state" of people who have a hard time speaking is established through it. This is either because they are shy or have an insufficient vocabulary or a slower spirit, which, by the way, has nothing to do with intelligence.

These simple questions of aptitudes make it so that some of us don't say what we think about the questions that concern us. What's more serious is that they would not be able to reach — even from their own standpoint — their own true opinion, which needs to associate freely with other people's opinions.

There's a risk that this will lead to two kinds of disunity. The first one results from what people should contribute that hasn't yet been contributed. The second one results from the fact that what some people have contributed hasn't been able to be unanimously assimilated into the common good. This leads to the stifling of certain tendencies.

I don't mean to say that what each of us thinks is good. Wanting to adopt *everyone's* opinions is a pleasant utopia. Refusing to do this isn't oppressive. But it is oppressive when some people are less free to express their way of thinking than others, and when this unexpressed thought will make phony meetings out of the group's organic meetings.

Mutual Christian Obedience

The opposite of the spirit of power is the spirit of obedience to others. It's a loving obedience for the good of others.

We'll talk elsewhere about the great obedience. It's the one that re-establishes the order of our relationships as creatures and as children in relation to God through the Church.

But if the love of God gives rise to our obedience as children of God, fraternal charity requires small acts of obedience from one person to another. Community life helps us become accustomed to this small constant obedience. It's a habit we'll have to preserve with all our brothers and sisters.

To be "the servants of one another," "the last ones," and "those who humble themselves" — all this isn't fiction or myth. It's mutual Christian obedience. It's also nothing more than acts of goodwill, asking God for the obedience that He alone gives and which the Church talks to us about all throughout Holy Week. "Christ became obedient to death, even death on a cross."

We can prepare ourselves for this sacrificial obedience that makes us recognize all of God's rights over us in the following way. We can acknowledge that we have no right over anyone. We can also recognize that we must accept being treated as if everyone had — not all the rights over us — but was *entitled to us* and entitled to this "greater love that is to give one's life for those we love."

There's no traditional vow of humility. It would be a huge deception. There's human poverty and obedience, even if what Christ did with them is beyond us. We can at least beg for their human aspect.

But humility is the *result* of God's mystery over us if we can be aware of it. It's the ordering of who we are before God the Creator, Savior, and Father. Everything in God that continues to be mysterious for us and that we only know through faith is somewhat equivalent to humility, which is also only acquired through a life of faith.

This is why, whatever form it takes, *humility is the invisible basis of every missionary* life. It is the only thing that can bring God to those who don't believe in Him.

This is why if we must cherish humility as all those who tried to be Christians cherished it, simply because God loves us, and we want to try to love Him. We must also cherish it in another way. It's because this is the condition of someone who adores Him, and so we owe it to God. The world owes it more than ever because it's the ultimate act of missionary reparation.

Finally, this is why every arrogant act of ours, of whatever kind, must be fought, denounced, and purified in us, as it hurts both God and people. This is why every circumstance — regardless of its origin, which may bring us humiliation, without causing us to harm others — must be accepted by us at once in silence, without our persisting in searching for a human explanation for it.

It's better to rejoice that, if we search deep within ourselves, we can find a way to love God in our humiliation. In the face of humiliation, we can even hope for an increase in its value that will nurture whomever God wants.

The Beatitudes and the Cross[21]

JESUS GIVES THE FIRST great guidelines of evangelical life in the Sermon on the Mount, which begins with the Beatitudes.

The Beatitudes have been our first outline of the way. We've used them to introduce ourselves to the whole sermon, which continues to be the practical foundation of what our life is about. It's a foundation we always return to in order to perfect it, for we're continually mixing a lot of sand with a few stones.

Giving the gift of our lives to the Lord without doing it joyfully would, at first, be a reason to doubt that this beginning really coincides with God's will.

We really know that.

What we perhaps know less, which risks disturbing us some day, is when it's no longer an issue of starting, but of continually returning to our point of departure — to the Sermon on the Mount's great texts. We understand both how they want us to live and how far we fall short of their commandments. What we know less is that joy could have left them all at once or little by little. Often, it could seem that even when

---

[21] Notes written for the intention of her teams, 1956.

the prayers we've made for the Beatitudes have been partly answered, this only arouses feelings of disgust in us. They will cover us in the face of this apparent duplicity between our first undertaking and this sort of rejection of what we've asked for. We have to be ready ahead of time for this experience, even if joy preserves its clarity for us.

We must know that the Beatitudes aren't bliss. "Come and share your master's joy" is said to the good servant when he's done serving. This joy is bliss. It's not fragile and has no eclipse. The joy in people's hearts is fragile and intermittent.

The Beatitudes are the absolute opposite of what people call joy. They continue to be contradictory as soon as we isolate them from faith. Each one carries either its cross or the threat of a cross, which is weighty, tangible, and indisputable. But every one of them also carries hope, which is only the hope of something invisible or good that occurs in the future. But the cross is never completed as long as it's not a mystery for us.

If all the great evangelical virtues can, with God's grace, be implemented through our goodwill, they only belong to Jesus when His Spirit fully communicates them by giving them a new dimension through the Cross and only through the Cross.

Christians pray in many ways in front of their crucifixes. They respect and contemplate them more or less often, and place themselves in their schools and homes. But once a year on Good Friday, the Church summons Christians to a liturgical prayer that's called neither a tribute, nor attention to, nor a lesson on the Cross. It's called the *Adoration of the Cross*. The cross is gradually uncovered for the faithful. *They are summoned to adore a veiled cross at the beginning of the service.*

This veiled cross waits for us if we want to be the beneficiaries of the Beatitudes. The cross, whose mere sign repels evil, surprises us so much that it risks tempting us.

We usually recognize the cross — whether to accept or reject it, whether to merely acquiesce to it or willingly take it up. But one day, or even for several years, it stands veiled before us, and we don't recognize it.

It's veiled by something that removes its form, shape, and size for us. It could seem to be made with incoherent phenomena or appear to come out like the phony shadow of a phony light. It could also force us to go the other way around. The mystery it offers us as soon as it approaches us *denies* a vital part of our human being — even of our Christian being. When it comes to appearances, the mystery of the Cross absolutely *mortifies* us — something that's essential for our lives, without which we couldn't act like human beings. In reality, it devastates one of those things that makes us the person we are.

If all the Beatitudes and virtues Jesus Christ taught, the advice He gave, and the promises He made each carry within them an access to the mystery of the Cross, it's because the entire good news is the good news of love. This was made possible for us and continues to be possible for us through the Cross and in the Cross.

The whole gospel is for love, but without the Cross that contains the very name of Jesus, we'd be strangers to love, which would be very contradictory. If, by our participation in the very life of Jesus, we can, in truth, participate in His love without participating in the Cross of Jesus and without the willingness to accept what this participation will be for each of us, then love will stay in us like a withered seed.

To belong to God, we have to experience a double-edged sword — joy and the cross.

To gloss over the contradictions which that presents in one's life and the tangible difficulties that ensue from it would be to be very optimistic about what we can expect from ourselves. We all have an ability to misrepresent and divide others and ourselves.

It would be easy for us to choose one or the other. Sometimes, in the name of joy, we don't take any suffering upon ourselves, no matter how mild it is. Sometimes, in the name of the cross, we emphasize the difficulties and sorrows which surround human existence in such an original manner, and we have joy take a leave so that we can be sorrowful, regretful, and bitter.

Or if we understand the inseparability of the cross and joy, we rather easily become the counterfeiters of joy and the cross, and do it even more easily if we have a "public."

We perhaps haven't always had the opportunity to see what a life that became a sacrifice for God looks like, because it seems that such a life is hardly ever noticed. On the other hand, who among us — believers as well as nonbelievers — have had the advantage of living with a victim? What family, work group, artistic sector, administration, or convent doesn't have its own? We are generally lucky that it doesn't let itself be ignored. I say lucky because without it, we never would have guessed that the person was a victim. A sacrifice isn't performed. But being sacrificed is an admirable role, and who doesn't find himself playing it at some point? This person could be the sacrificed husband, brother, sister, friend, genius, or saint. Let him joyfully sacrifice himself. This is the hero.

If we don't love ridicule and if acting like a victim isn't our way of doing things, we'll very rarely completely escape not playing the role during the trials of our lives. Who among us, when he is in a lot of pain, doesn't forget to think that he could perhaps be being punished like a child by God our Father instead of seeing it as reparation for the sins of others or a test of our own fidelity? Who among us in some public trials — while trying to reconcile joy and the cross — has been less interested in giving our neighbor a perfect testimony than in gently receiving the joy and the cross from God?

All this can be done by us with joy and the cross, as it is by others.

Some convictions can prevent us from making mistakes:

✠ The Lord will give us *His* Cross — the one that fully unites us to Him only if we have tried with all our strength and for love of Him to wholeheartedly receive the suffering, worries, and setbacks in our lives.

✠ But He can't give His generous, gratuitous Cross to those of who haven't willingly and a little gratuitously suffered out of love for Him.

✠ The Lord can crush us under His Cross so that we don't recognize it. This forces us to scream or struggle. But that must not prevent us from looking for even the smallest grain of dust that we could offer Him in joy.

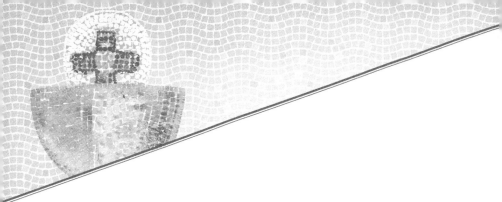

The Christian, an Unusual Person[22]

To THE EXTENT THAT a Christian professes his faith and tries to live it, he becomes unusual to believers and unbelievers.

This is because the Gospel won't stop being the good news for Jews and Gentiles until the end of time.

The unusualness of the Christian is purely and simply his resemblance to Jesus Christ, which is put into a person at Baptism and crosses through his heart as if it goes all the way to his skin.

This resemblance entails Christ's very characteristics — just as two eyes, a nose, and a mouth make up a person's face, regardless of this person's age, mentality, or color.

This resemblance has to do with Christ's characteristics. It includes those who are intelligent and foolish, who suffer a little and a lot, and who are great and little, according to the world.

Being unusual does not mean being a remarkable person, which somehow entitles one to be a "Christian." It's the refusal or denunciation in one's own life of everything that can sever one's resemblance to

---

[22] A personal note written in 1962 after, so it seems, a meeting where there had been an issue of defining the characteristics of today's Christian.

Jesus Christ. It's not the shining achievement of a Christian that makes him unusual. It's the fact that Christ — who is always the same — shows His face through the face of a human being.

He not only believes in God; he must love Him as a son loves a loving and all-powerful Father, as Christ loved Him.

He's not only dependent upon God; he is supremely free through God's will.

He not only loves his neighbor as himself; he must love the neighbor "as Christ loved us" — in Christ's own way.

He's not only a brother; he is a good brother — in words and deeds. There are no limits or dispensations from this goodness.

He's not only a brother to his next-door neighbor; he is a brother to his neighbor on the other side of the earth.

He's not only a legal brother; he is a practical brother who is straight to the point. He's not condescending or distant. He's everyone's neighbor and neither lowers himself nor becomes haughty and aloof. He's on the same level. He has no privileges or rights and is superior to no one.

Not only does he give, he also shares. He lends something without expecting it to be returned. He's available not only to do what is asked of him, but more than what is asked of him.

He's not only without lies but without silences and "added explanations."

He's not only a brother to those who love him, but also to his enemies. He not only tolerates being struck; he doesn't flee from the one who strikes him.

Not only does he refuse to return evil for evil, he forgives and forgets the evil. Not only does he forget the evil, he returns it with goodness.

He not only suffers and is put to death by some; he dies while suffering for them — not only once, but every time.

He not only judges justly; he doesn't judge anyone.

He not only shares what he has or what's in him; he gives the only thing that God has given him as his own — his own life.

He not only fights against the evil within himself; he fights the evil outside of himself. He not only fights against evil wherever it is, but against its fruits — misfortune, suffering, and death. But he fights with goodness and without sinning. If it's a question of the happiness of many people, he doesn't accept paying for it via the misfortune of one person.

He not only combats evil in the world; he accepts the suffering he must undergo.

He not only accepts suffering; he accepts it willingly and deliberately, because in it resides the Christian struggle's energy, effectiveness, and weapon.

He not only struggles; he struggles without glory so that God Himself would be glorified, in order that His name be sanctified and His reign expedited.

He agrees not to look like a hero and not to be one. He accepts not only not being admired; he rejoices in being ignored — not only that others won't esteem him, but even that he won't esteem himself.

He not only puts all his energy into his task, but he doesn't ask what his task is for. He not only doesn't know who started it; he ignores the work of God in which it's used.

He not only struggles, but is peaceful, because the omnipotent and loving God who started it is always the one who powerfully and lovingly finishes it. With unwavering confidence, he expects God to provide him with what he works for with all his strength, that his strength alone could never achieve. He asks God that His will be done. He expects God's Kingdom to come from Him. He knows that prayer is the energy of action.

He not only loves life because God created it; he is happy to experience a life that's eternal for everyone.

He's not only happy to live, but is happy to die, because dying is being born to eternal life, and everyone will be judged by God's love and God's loving justice. He's happy to live, not only because creation is God's daughter, but because her beauty is indestructible even when it's botched. He's happy to live, not only because man is overwhelmed by God's goodness, but because God allows evil only to bring forth a better good.

He not only acts in time, but waits for the fruits of eternity, whose seed he sows in time. This is what he calls hope.

He's not only happy because he lives, thanks to God, but because he'll help his brothers and sisters to live with God forever.

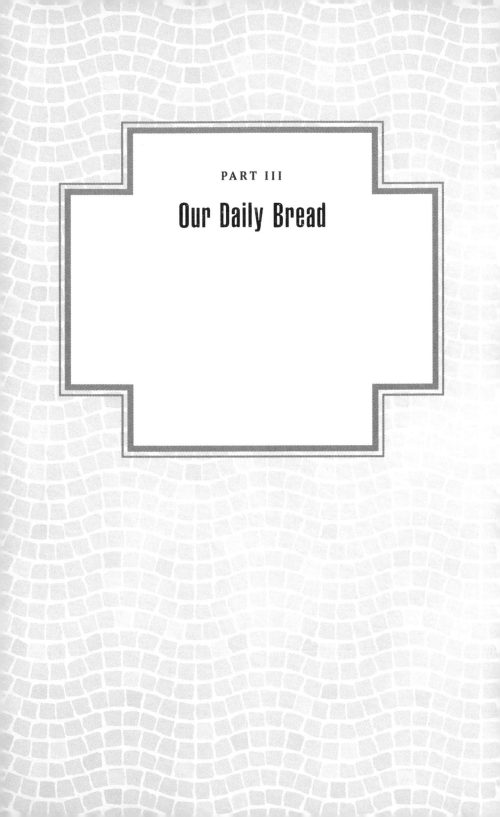

PART III

Our Daily Bread

Lord, teach us the role
that the unique dance of our obedience
holds in this eternal novel
written by You.

Reveal to us the grand orchestra
of your designs, or let what you permit
cast strange notes into the serenity
of what you desire.

We, the Ordinary People of the Streets.

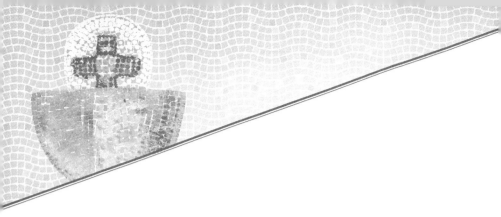

Six Meditations on Daily Life

The Ecstasy of Your Will

WHEN THOSE WE LOVE ask us for something, we thank them for having asked us.

If it would please you, Lord, to ask us one thing in our whole lives, we'd still be amazed. To have done Your will this one time would be the single event that determined our destiny.

But because You put such an honorable task in our hands every minute of every hour of every day, we find this so natural that we're bored by it.

And yet, if we understood to what extent Your mystery is unthinkable, we'd continue to be amazed at these sparks of Your will that our miniscule tasks are made up of. We'd be awed to know the innumerable, precise, and personal illuminations of Your will in this great darkness that covers us.

On the day we understand this, we'll go through life as some kind of prophet — like those who see the tiny workings of Your Providence and those who intervene for You. Nothing will be mediocre, because You'll want everything. Nothing will be too heavy, because everything will be rooted in You. Nothing will be sad, because You'll desire everything. Nothing will be boring, because everything will be done out of love for You.

We're all predestined to be ecstatic, to get out of our poor connections, and rise up in Your plan hour after hour. We're never lamentable misfits, but blessed people who are called to know what You like to do and what You expect us to do in every moment. We are people who are needed by You, whose actions You would miss if we refused to do them. This includes darning the cotton ball, writing the letter, getting the child out of bed, cheering our husband up, opening the door, answering the phone, and enduring the headache. There are so many springboards to ecstasy and so many bridges to get across from my poor ill will to the serene shore of Your good pleasure.

Ease

It's very painful to love You without being joyful, You whom we think to be our joy. It grieves us to hang on to Your will, which moves us every day without ease and grace.

Our greatest sorrow, O Lord, is to hear an artist play the music of mankind, being carried away by it effortlessly, encountering through the acrobatics of harmony a wave of love that is merely human in scale.

Perhaps he needs to teach us to play Your love — we for whom this love is too big and heavy.

I saw a man who was playing a Gypsy song on a wooden violin with hands that were made of flesh. His heart and the music met in the violin. Those who listened to him could never have guessed that this song was hard and that he had to follow the scales for a long time, crush his fingers, and let the notes and sounds sink into the fibers of his memory.

His body hardly moved — except for his fingers and arms.

If he had worked to possess his knowledge of music for a long time, the music now possessed and animated him, and projected him outside of himself — like an enchanting sound.

We could discern a deep history of practice, effort, and struggle within each note that he played.

Every one of the notes fled, as if its role had ended when it had traced the path of another perfect note through a sound that was accurate, precise, and perfect. Each note lasted as long as it needed to and not a second longer. None of them left too quickly nor lingered. They served an imperceptible and all-powerful spirit.

I saw some poor, anxious artists playing pieces that were too hard for them. Their playing showed everyone the trouble they took to do this. We had a hard time hearing their music because we were so distracted by their awkward movements and palpable anxiety.

It's very painful to play Your beautiful music without joy, Lord — You who move us from day to day. It's quite painful to continue practicing, and our efforts are lacking in grace. It's extremely painful that people think that we're burdened, overly serious, and abused.

It's very painful to be unable to spread the ease of eternity in our corner of the world amidst our work, haste, and fatigue.

The Passion of Patience

We are waiting for our passion. We know it must come, and we agree that we intend to experience it with a certain grandeur.

We're waiting for the bell to ring for us to sacrifice ourselves.

We know we must be consumed like a log in the fire. We must be separated like a woolen thread that's cut with scissors. We must be destroyed like a young cow headed for slaughter.

We're waiting for our passion, and it doesn't come.

Patience is what comes.

Patience consists of small pieces of passion whose job it is to slay us gently for Your glory, without reserving any glory for ourselves.

They come to us in the morning.

They are our nerves that are vibrating too much or are too soft, the bus that goes by because it's full, the milk that boils over, the chimney sweeps who arrive, the children who mix everything up, the guests our husband brings over, this friend who doesn't come, the phone that doesn't stop ringing, and those we love who no longer love us in return. It's feeling like being quiet and having to talk. It's feeling like talking when we have to be quiet. It's wanting to go out when we ought to stay in. It's staying in when we feel like going out. It's the husband we'd like to lean on who becomes the most fragile child. It's the disgust with our daily portion, and the anxious desire for everything that isn't ours.

Thus, our patience comes in serried ranks and single file. It forgets to tell us that it is the martyrdom that was prepared for us.

We scornfully let it go by and wait for an opportune moment.

For we have forgotten that if there are branches that are destroyed by the fire, there are boards that our footsteps slowly wear out which fall into thin sawdust.

We've forgotten that if there are yarns of wool that are cut outright with scissors, there are yarns for knitting that slim down from day to day on the backs of those who wear them. If every redemption is a martyrdom, every martyrdom isn't bloody. There are some that are strung out from one end of life to the other.

This is the passion of patience.

The New Day

Another day is starting.

Jesus wants to live it in me. He hasn't shut Himself out. He walked among people. He's with me among the people I encounter today.

He'll meet all those who come into the house. He'll also meet all those I see on the street — rich people different than the ones who lived when He was on the earth, poor people, scholars and simple-tons, children and elderly people, saints and sinners, able-bodied and disabled people.

All of them will be people He's come looking for — those He's come to save.

He'll respond to those who talk to me. He'll have something to give those who don't have much. Each person will exist for Him as if he were alone. He'll experience His silence in the cacophony and bring about His peace in the midst of chaos.

Jesus hasn't stopped being the Son. He wants to stay connected to the Father in me — gently linked in every second, balanced in every second like a cork on the water, gentle like a lamb before every one of His Father's wishes.

Everything will be permitted on the day now dawning. All will be allowed and will require that I say yes. The world He left me in to be with me can't prevent me from being with God — just like an in-fant who is carried in his mother's arms isn't with her any less be-cause she's walking in the crowd.

Jesus is still everywhere. We can't prevent ourselves from being God's representatives at any moment.

Jesus is present throughout this day, which we share with the people of our time and of all time — both those of my city and the whole world.

Through the brothers and sisters who are close to us, whom He will make us to serve, love, and save, waves of His love will go out to the end of the world and the end of time.

Blessed be this new day, which is Christmas for the earth, since Jesus wants to live it in me again.

You'll Die from Death

People in convents often prepare for death.

We don't have time to do this. But we are wisely prepared anyway.

Life prepares us for death. It really knows its job. You just have to listen to it, follow it, and see it.

It prepares us for death slightly or extensively, depending on the day. Sometimes it does this without harming us at all. Other times, it does it by breaking up the pain. Sometimes it does this by stressing our little daily deaths. Other times, it does this by spreading death to those we love more than ourselves.

We are reminded of death when we comb our hair in the morning and find that our hair is getting thin, when the toothache we've had for a long time leaves us, when our skin creases in the corners of our eyes, and when we can say — while talking about some tidbits of memories — "Ten, twenty, or thirty years ago ..." Death comes to us when people come with flowers every year to wish us a happy birthday — flowers that remind us of a cemetery and that celebrate one less year to live on this earth.

Death is there in each reunion with those who preserve our childhood and among whom we continue to be children. We learn about death when our memories unravel and when we suffer physically. Death occupies these human areas in advance.

Each time we return to the place we grew up, the list of visits to the living gets shorter and the visit among the tombs longer.

We are faced with death when we're finally torn from our loved ones. Even when faith and the hope that we'll be reunited and our love for them affirms our joy that they have gone back home, we stay on with our blood that protests, our flesh that's grown hollow and has been hurt (a large piece of which seems to have been destroyed). We remain with this horror of the dark cold earth, which made even Jesus cry. Death is discovered some evening between our rising and our retiring. It reveals that it's on the lookout and lurks in our depths. It blows in our faces as if to tame us, and we're surprised that we need so much courage.

We don't need to be a poet to learn about death — each night and each October — with the old dog that has to be put down and those strange little bodies of mice and lizards that are flattened by car wheels on the roads.

Life teaches us about death. But in turn, death teaches us about life — we who know about human repentance.

As a mother suffers from childbirth, and the father sweats to feed the child who is living, so we bear our deaths that have started and are almost finished in our own and final creation. But we must be properly born each time we die, born a little when we die a little and born a lot when we die a lot. This is about learning to spend time with life by spending time with death. It is a matter of turning toward the eternal, like the negatives of photographic films, where the image is captured and all the blacks become white.

We have to open our eyes of faith when our own eyes fail us.

Just as we're not dismayed by the yellowing of a blade of grass when we look at our garden, let's be interested enough in this century and beyond, so that the time of our lives doesn't matter to us and everything we love is transferred into a calm eternity. Thus, we'll learn to die to death in order to live authentically.

Zeroes and Infinity[23]

We can't believe in both coincidence and God. We believe in Providence. We live as if we believe in coincidence. The inconsistency of our lives, its unhealthy turmoil and passivity, originates from this false belief.

We endure what we haven't chosen. These are our zeroes — the zero of the job that's required of us, of friends we're forced to be with, the zero of our anonymous clientele and of our professional visits. Zero! Zero! Zero!

---

[23] A text that was published in *Offertoire* [*Offertory*] magazine, 1953.

In other circumstances, meetings, and tasks, we assign ratings of two, five, and seven to the divine will, according to how we feel about these circumstances, meetings, and tasks. We focus our greatest energies there, as if that's where our life started.

Yet every morning we receive our entire day from God's hands. God gives us a day that He prepares for us. It contains nothing that's excessive, insufficient, unimportant, or useless. It's a masterpiece of a day that He asks us to experience. We look at it as if it were an agenda sheet that's marked with a number and a month. We treat it lightly, like a sheet of paper. If we could search the world and see this day develop and be formed from the beginning of time, we'd understand the import of a single human day.

And if we had a little faith, we'd feel like kneeling before the day we're experiencing as Christians.

We're charged with energies that are disproportionate to the measures of the world — faith that knocks mountains over, hope that believes the impossible, and love that makes the earth blaze.

Each minute of the day — regardless of what it calls us to be or do — allows Christ to live in us among people. So, it's no longer a question of calculating the effectiveness of our time.

Our zeroes multiply infinity.

We humbly take on the dimensions of God's will.

Our Daily Bread[24]

THERE ARE CHRISTIANS WHO climb Paradise. Some of them are earthlings. They wait for Paradise to shape them such that they might fit in through its cracks.

The scale of Paradise within us is the meticulous and magnanimous fulfillment of our daily duty; this duty is the opposite of what one could call the spirit of movement, of searching.

It hands over the little fragment of humanity that we are, which establishes us in a loving order to God's visitation.

Carrying out our daily task is accepting where we are so that the Kingdom of God comes to us and expands on this part of the earth that we call home.

It's to accept — as a large act of obedience — the matter that we're made of, the family we belong to, the profession in which we work, our people, the Continent, the world that surrounds us, and the time in which we're living.

24 A text that was published in the "Rencontres" ["Encounters"] collection: *Contemplation*, 1941.

For the duty of our station in life isn't this petty obligation that we sometimes talk about. It's the debt we owe as carnal children, fathers, civil servants, bosses, workers, storekeepers, French people, Europeans, and "world citizens" who are living in 1941.

What makes one righteous is the payment of a debt that's completely paid one penny at a time each second.

Going around a task that's envisioned in this way would be a great trip. We'd just go through some of the steps we want to take.

Our Bodies

Our state or being has to do with possessing a body. Our body is the first thing we encounter when we wake up in the morning. It's not always pleasant, and its condition, sometimes cordial and sometimes stormy, will follow us throughout the day. How many of us — when we're overloaded or tempted — haven't had a great desire to curse our bodies and almost ask to be freed of them. Yet our body isn't a coincidence. God wanted it and measured it out. We have nerves, blood, and a deep temperament that He wanted for us. God fashioned our bodies in advance in order for His grace to live in them. He's not unaware of any weakness, compromising behavior, or deviation. But He chose to make it into the body of a saint.

We have the body of our destiny and holiness.

Our body is the place where incidents occur throughout the day that often make war with our soul — the tremor of our nerves, our headaches, our good or bad dispositions. There are so many small circumstances that are nonetheless circumstances that express God's will for us. None of that is something negative that has to revolt or embarrass us. On the contrary, all of it entails God's coming to us. It's a bit of His will that becomes clear to us. This peace of mind, this migraine and these tired legs, are our temporal blessing.

We should get used to managing our bodies. The body is the life that God entrusts us with. We must discard the notion that we own it and rediscover that it is His. We should face our bodies in the same way that a peasant faces his land. We need to know what our bodies are worth and assess them. We need to know the body's riches and flaws, what strengthens and weakens it. We also need to try to harmonize it with those great natural laws that God invented, which we mention when we want to represent the union of redeemed souls with Christ.

Our bodies don't stop at boundaries that are easily perceptible to us. In this time when medical and psychological studies often crudely shed light on our heredities, many people can be disturbed. They can feel hurt and shaken by these inner surges, tastes, instincts, characteristics, passions, and imbalances in their desire for spiritual integrity. Yet this human mass is also the material life of grace — the vessel that grace operates in and through. God also decided to use it to make saints out of us. Nothing in it is disturbing because everything is provided for. It's a joy to offer God this piece of humanity, which has been passed down to us from the depths of both pure and guilty forebears, as a voluntary service, to be its keeper and be empowered to make it holy.

It's exciting to know that our will, when it's attached to God's will, is enough for all this mass of humanity to be in order. Our will must be stretched and gentle — stretched toward God and unraveled from its own rigidity like a well-tanned skin sheath that is put on a blade and becomes hard like that which it encases.

This discovery of God's will in our bodies means that we must respectfully consider the least morsel. We have to be reverent toward what God has created. We don't need to fear materializing our lives in this way. This reverence that we'll give to God's action in our bodies will lead us to a deep adoration of the work He's carrying out in our spirits. The justice we'll practice toward our bodies will perhaps make us more just toward our souls.

Our Daily Suffering

No suffering is accidental.

Our daily bread is given to us through the daily suffering of our brothers and sisters. It's our daily grace, and there's always a little portion in our daily graces that comes from someone's daily suffering somewhere.

No suffering is a fluke. Only our will is random. We don't always want our suffering, and we skimp on it, haggle over it, and botch it.

Just as there's work that's done well, we might also say that there is suffering that is done well.

When we get up in the morning, we have both our suffering and our work cut out for us. The details of our work are willed by God, as are the details of our suffering. We can do our work very well and suffer badly. We can easily control and verify the deficiencies in our work.

We'll know about the irreparable ruptures that the deficiencies of our pain caused in the structure of grace only after our death.

When we do God's will, when we get up, prepare a meal, go out, shop, and catch our train, we go into a union with the Lord, so to speak, by accepting and wanting His will.

When we struggle with daily suffering, when we get up and our legs are so sore that they give out, when we need ten times as many steps, ten times as much time, and ten times as many nerves to prepare the simplest of meals, when we have to cook with smoke in our eyes from bad coal that doesn't emit any heat while standing barefoot on freezing cobblestones....

When we leave our warm rooms to go on the street to skate on the ice, and while stumbling and ploughing through the snow, we tour the city to bring back our most modest purchases....

When we wait for a train that's not coming on a platform where we're cold....

In any and all of these things, we become donors of God's grace through our suffering, while simultaneously being integrated into His will.

You'll say that all of these are small sufferings. But we recognize an artist just as well in the way he plays a children's piece as when he plays in a very difficult concert.

Thus, we'll quickly recognize a saint in all these small sufferings. He experiences them naturally, with ease and grace — in both senses of the word. It's a good grace that makes a large work of love out of this small suffering.

We must love greatly to experience our suffering elegantly. We have to wear our pain well, in the way people say that one wears a piece of clothing well, a sweater that doesn't bother you and is tailored just for you — in which you're at ease.

We wear our suffering like social climbers. We play it like a musical piece that's too hard, becoming tense and looking at the notes without any sense of style.

This devotion to God in our small pains will preserve us from two faults that we're often tempted to commit against the spirit of the earth we talked about earlier.

The first of these faults is to look beyond our familiar horizon for ways of redeeming our world, which is so desperately in need of redemption. The daily balance of this redemption that each of us owes is found in our portion of daily suffering. The exact count will be there.

The second fault is to let ourselves be trapped by our exterior actions, to evaluate them according to their outer surface without first assuring ourselves that this surface is rooted in the divine will, to evaluate our exterior actions without measuring them by the depth of their suffering.

These are our truly effective and universal actions. They connect us to the powerful sap that is found in the Holy Rood, and make us present to everyone who still needs to be saved.

Finally, our small sufferings are the marvelous means we have to stimulate the world's great suffering and make it bear fruit. Nothing is as sad at this time as seeing the whole world blindly going through such exceptional trials.

Yet these daily trials are apportioned to each of us. It's such a great joy to know that by willing each of our small sufferings, we become the eyes of the sorrowful, groping world.

Sometimes, one colorful vase highlights all the tones in a room that have the same color, which had been imperceptible before. We start thinking that while God is looking at the world, because He sees a little goodwill shining, He accepts the group's bleak passivity as a sacrifice that's worthy of being approved.

A little bit of suffering that's accepted hands a soul over to volumes of incredible universal suffering. Through our suffering, we help the world to do its penance.

Have we, who are so fond of news, and so quick to interpret it optimistically or pessimistically, considered that botching a small piece of our daily suffering and balking before the sunrise — in front of this tasteless food and this numbing cold — is more important for the world's history than some disaster or victory that we hear about on the radio?

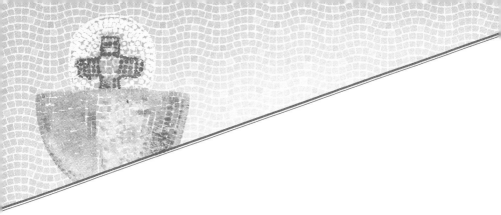

Notes

The Will of God 1950

JUST BECAUSE GOD WANTS us to do certain things, we must not confuse these things in themselves with God's will. God's will, and not the things which His will requires us to do, must remain the goal of our own individual wills.

"Those who are led by the Spirit of God are children of God."

"Those who are born of the Spirit do not know from where they are coming or to where they are going."

Our work — our task — is to do God's will, and God's will is only carried out in faith.

All the actions that God's will asks of us, which activate our natural abilities, are only valid, as far as this goes, if they are animated by faith and are acts of faith. The proof that they are acts of faith is whether we can make pure acts of faith — as soon as they are asked of us — in which reason, logic, and understanding are sacrificed.

In order for all our actions to be used for the world's salvation and for them to have the potential to evangelize — even when we're cooking or eating with someone — they need to be filled with faith, a faith that's just as necessary then as it would be if we sought to raise the dead.

...And the Word of God   1964

Events can only be signs of God's will if we connect them with the Word of God and put it in them. Then, the Word will reveal God's will, which must be sought in the very foundation of these events.

God's Word is altogether an unchanging law of life. It's a leaven of life, a mobile and rapid guide that enables us to live.

To know what we have to do, let us not ask for "signs and wonders" before having gone through the Word of God. He doesn't say it once and for all, all in advance. We will never finish understanding what He always tells us. What He tells us each day is His resounding Word, located in the events and circumstances that each of us encounters in our daily lives.

The Word of God that's listened to, heard, kept, and given *does* God's will in and through us. It's active and effective, and continually creates and recreates.

This is valid for every Christian life.

In creating life, God didn't create an inert monument. He created a life that was growing, dynamic, evolving, lively, and fruitful. Every life that's born from the Word of God — a Word that is endlessly creative — is growing, dynamic, evolving, lively, and fruitful. It's a life that's destined for eternal life. It's a life that's always contemporary and grafted onto the movement of time.

The Church's growth is connected to the growth of the Word of God. Welcoming the Word of God and letting ourselves grow through it is participating in and working for God's Church.

For the fruitfulness of God's Word must be conveyed. Its transmission is inseparable from contradiction and the cross.

Every Christian life is based on faith, which is to say God's Word — the indisputable Word of the undisputed Lord.

The Bridegroom Is the One Who Has the Bride[25]

I THINK JUST ABOUT all of us need to return more concretely to the Lord Jesus — to return to Him through close relationships that are His relationships in the Church.

We need to review our lives as lives of women who are offered to Him. That is to say:

- ✣ to learn to love Jesus with a personal, active, and intimate love. This love is called *prayer*.
- ✣ to learn the responsibilities of the work of Jesus Christ. This love, which must be active in a world that has been given by Jesus, has the duty to fulfill these responsibilities. This love is also called *goodness*.
- ✣ to learn the fruitfulness of those whom Jesus Christ possesses. This love must be proclaimed, offered, and obtained. This love is also called *suffering*.

We essentially need to learn to be the Lord's women in and with the Church. It's the feminine equivalent of "man of God."

[25] A note written for her teams, 1953.

I'm haunted by the dual mystery through which our lives must pass — the mystery of love and the mystery of the Church. The Bride of Christ in the Church is each person, each of whom is called to love Him. Each baptized person participates in this conjugal love. We've agreed to be satisfied with this love alone, as have religious and consecrated people. If we don't devote our whole being to Him, or if we don't give Him what is His by right, we're of no help in spreading life — including eternal life.

At the beginning of the New Testament, John the Baptist said: "It is the bridegroom who has the bride, but the friend of the bridegroom rejoices."

Nonbelievers who are better than us and Christians who are better than us haven't been called to live in the fullness of the mystery of the Church, the Bride of Christ. They are like the friend who rejoices. We might be tempted to be mistaken about our vocation and take the vocation of the friend.

Whatever the husband gives His friends — trust, confidences, and responsibilities — he gives his name to his wife alone, so that she'll be what he is, do what he does, and transmit his own life through her. It's not because she goes on the streets to shop — where his friends are — that she's his wife. The maid can do that. It's because she dines with her husband and spends the night with him.

Being the Bride is different from being in the world in the way that the Son of God, who was sent into the world and grafts us on the Church as the Bride, was in the world. Being the Bride is constantly leaving the night of the theological mystery of love and going from it to the world.

It's not working with her husband that makes a woman his wife. His friends work just like she does, and sometimes better. It's being entirely possessed by him. What she earns is doubly his because *she* is his.

It's not doing this or that job perfectly or practicing a particular profession that grafts us into union with the Church. It's being so driven by Christ that this action of ours in the world is really His.

The bride isn't the bride because she can tidy up the home. A hotel owner could do this very well. Before living in the home, her husband's children lived in her flesh, because she bore them and fed them from herself.

We won't be grafted in marriage to the Church by organizing the world. Rather, we are grafted by carrying along everyone in this world, every person we meet. It's not in organizing their lives for them, but in giving them the right to live in our lives and communicating all that we are with them and all that we have — from bread to grace.

A mother isn't a mother because she gives gifts to her children. Friends can make them gifts just as well. She's a mother because she gives them her husband's life at the same time as her own.

It's not giving people happiness that makes us the Bride of Christ. Rather, it consists in giving them eternal life, the very life of God. We're terribly adulterous if we give our children the life of the world.

In raising her children, the mother prepares for the future. She doesn't prepare them for an eternal childhood of toys and candy.

We're responsible for these eternal beings, and if we only give them comfort and entertainment, we're like a mother who builds her children's future with baby clothes.

The wife must establish her life where her husband has established his.

Jesus Christ doesn't live in the world's powers. He was the child of a declining family among an ancient and minor people. He was neither a Roman citizen, holder of the keys to the world's empire, nor a barbarian, who would build tomorrow's empire, nor a Greek, who had the empire of the spirit, nor a slave who had the strength of the oppressed masses. He lived and continues to live in the world's weakness.

The wife has the same living conditions as her husband.

Jesus Christ lives in peace and not in tranquility because He is merciful, and the one who gives everyone what he lacks is never finished with His work.

The bride is not a fiancée who has time to walk on the dock and sit on the bench, idly daydreaming. She's the one who works like mad, keeps watch, and gives birth. She knows her husband better than she did when they were just young lovers. She knows his life by living her life.

But, at the same time, she knows her tasks and struggles. She doesn't ask him to think of her, but they think together.

With friends, you talk, speculate, and reminisce. The wife is not a friend.

Life is short, and the world calls out to be saved.

We have good times with our friends, and we come away from them feeling refreshed. The love of a husband for his wife gives her children, and she doesn't choose the way of bringing them into the world. She must suffer.

She doesn't give birth to works of art in euphoria and withdrawal, but to children of Adam, out of whom she makes children of God with her flesh and soul.

A friend knows the husband by looking at him and listening to him. The wife isn't a wife because she listens to her husband and looks at him, but because she knows him in a deeper way. The friend's eyes are perhaps better than hers, and his intelligence might better understand what the husband says. But he won't know what the wife knows.

That's what the Church knows, and what we know in her. It is our faith.

The friend can wait for the husband, but it is only his wife that desires and hopes for him. She doesn't expect anything from him. She hopes to become alive in other ways.

The Church's desire is hope, and she's so consumed by it that she can't want anything else.

The friend can be rich or poor. He can be free or enslaved. The wife can only be poor, and can only obey. Love for her is a poverty that only her husband can enrich. The child she bears and forms tears itself away from her and leaves her poor again. For her, love has to do with being obedient. She's passive in being fertile and giving birth.

The Church is the great poor and obedient person in the world, and we can't find love without poverty and obedience.

It's only by making a mistake about the distinction between the Kingdom of Heaven and the earthly city that we stop being connected to the Church as brides and become mere friends. It's only when poverty, obedience, or purity become objects in themselves and not conditions of love that we lose sight of our marital duties to the Church.

It happens when faith and hope, which are great resources for love — but which will pass — are experienced too weakly by us and leave us abandoned.

The friend is the one who creates something absolute with something relative, and we don't have the right to do this.

But if we agree to experience this simple and powerful vocation to love with and in the Church, we'll bear Jesus Christ's name for good. Everything we ask for in His name will be granted to us. We'll be effective in doing God's work with God's own power.

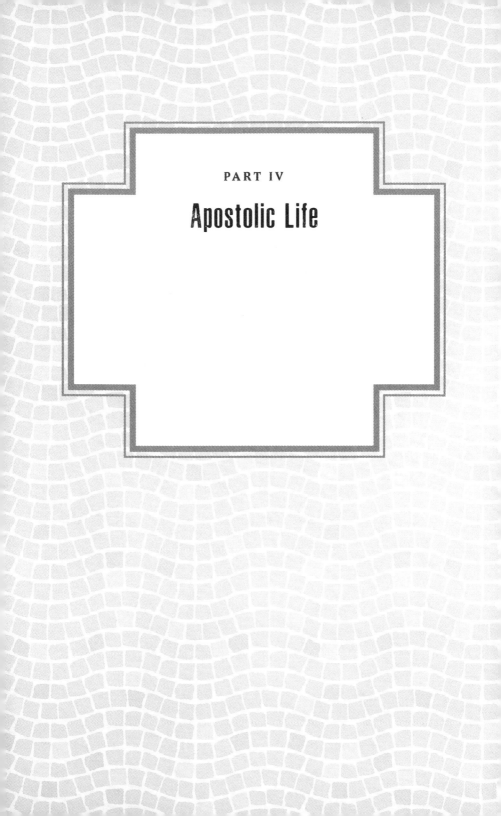

PART IV

Apostolic Life

The hope of the apostles of all times is a huge
begging woman who has her feet on a lost world.
Her arms are carrying the most befuddled people.
She shares their infinite poverty ... but she's
smiling at a redemption that she's awaiting
from Heaven, just as we're waiting for the day.

Unpublished text.

The Two Calls[26]

MISSIONARIES ARE MARKED BY a call, and this call is not always the same.

"Return home and give witness to what God has done for you."

The Lord already said this to someone who lived when He did, and He continues to say it to people in our time. He puts in their hearts such a love for their brothers and sisters that He encourages them to share their whole lives in a communion that is absolute.

They see society as the continuation of God's creation. They think that it is to be sanctified and purified, and that everything needs to be "brought together in Christ." They love one cell of the social body. Their vocation is to make this cell part of the Mystical Body.

They want to take everything that's not sinful in the world and transform it into a place of grace.

They will have a house that's just like the other houses — built in an orderly way that promotes peace — but full of tenderness. They will be peasants among peasants. Everything will have its price. They will be strong like others, ambitious for a better tomorrow.

---

[26] An excerpt from an unpublished text, *Missionaries sans bateaux* [*Missionaries Without a Boat*], 1943.

They will be working like all the others, with the same workdays in the same noise of the same workshops, observing the Sabbath on the same Sundays.

They will be with those who gave them life, surrounded by those to whom they have in turn given birth.

They will experience a faith that each of those they came to save can experience. They will experience it while thinking of them so that they can, in turn, experience it too.

They will experience it so beautifully, joyfully, and supernaturally that everyone will want to experience it with them.

They will be missionaries in the lands where they were born. They will be buried like a grain of wheat in the humility of their providential land.

They will build the heavenly Jerusalem in the streets of Paris, Lyons, and Lille, on the hills of Yonne, the plateaus of Eure, and the canal barges along the Rhine.

They will be where God put them from the beginning, like a little grain of seed from which a whole field could emerge. Nothing must separate them from the sinner, from the unbeliever they have come looking for in this mission, which simply asked them to stay where they were.

They will know that their missionary vessel could be the home they were born in.

After the missionaries of the homes, there are missionaries of the road, the street, and the lanes.

They encountered Christ on the road.

He was a poor Christ who didn't know where to place His head—a homeless Christ. He was a Christ who moved in His Father's will like a feather in the wind, a Christ without moorings who said to them: "Come, follow me."

They understood once and for all that Christ was their home.

"They follow the Lamb wherever He goes." It's as if they were possessed by a passion for sameness.

The others offer their lives, families, homes, and jobs so that the work of the Incarnation which Christ started would be built up in these spots. They are asking that everything about themselves would be wiped away, that Christ might cover them with the humanity that He experienced.

The former want Christ to be incarnated in all the realities of their lives. The latter ask to be clothed with Christ and nothing else.

The former are given a clearly defined apostolic task — to save the people of this profession, family, or place. To do this, they undertake everything that would get them closer to those they have to save. These people think that Christ's remedy from two thousand years ago must last to the end of the ages, that the small group that was poor, pure, and obedient like Him must have traveled all of the earth's roads before the Last Day will finally come.

This group must be renewed with each generation. The Lord has marked in advance those who are to imitate Him.

Since the gospel was first preached, many people who stayed in their homes have been disciples of Jesus Christ. Still others have had to leave their homes.

Many people peacefully possessed their property, received the Lord at their tables, and even did Him a great service. Yet others had to leave all they had to the poor and pursue paths that had no guaranteed outcomes.

The two roads have always existed.

The Lord will always tell some: "Because of Me and for My love, you'll have a wife, children, a home, and property to manage for me in the world."

The Lord will always say to others: "You'll only have Me, and I'll be everything for you."

The Lord will always say to some: "I know what suits you. I'll give you your suffering and daily bread every day, so that wherever you have settled down, my Cross will be there."

The Lord will always say to others: "Take up your cross, and follow Me. Take it up in the three arms of poverty, obedience, and purity. Why? Because this is how I want you to love Me and how we will love the world together."

Most of those Christ speaks to in this way wear brown, black, or white robes. They are disciples of a saint who was the Lord's road companion in ages past.

Others are people like you and me. They are people who have sunk as far as possible into the world's depths. They aren't separated from this world by any rule, vow, habit, or convent. They are poor, but like people from anywhere or nowhere. They are pure, but like people from any or no milieu.

They are obedient, but like people from any place or no place.

They are made for everything and for everyone. You'll find some who are going to school, others who are writing laws, others who heal and console, still others who work in factories.

For them, one world is as good as another world, and one person is as good as another one. But don't bore them with methods and techniques.

Don't tell them: "It's better to look a little rich here. You'll be better off," or "You should marry there. You'll be a better apostle," or "Know what you want, and hold on to it."

They will reply: "You can't follow two paths. You're giving us recipes that aren't for us."

If we're a bit worn out, and if we look like vagrants in this world, it's because our calling is to belong only to the Lord.

If we don't have a home, a husband, wife, or child who is waiting for us, it's because the Lord possesses us completely, and we Him alone to possess us.

If we have no program, it's because our Heavenly Father has written it for us in advance, and it's enough for us to receive His instructions day by day.

Don't tell them that the cross is dangerous, a little morbid, or unhealthy, or that the world needs to rediscover joy and rather than penance.

They will reply: "We'll talk to you about joy when we've learned it on the cross, where we'll rediscover our love. Our joy is so exorbitantly expensive that we had to sell all we had and all of ourselves in order to buy it."

Those of the first calling have to be numerous because the world is vast, and it takes a long time to baptize it.

But there must be at least a few of the second calling to offer people — these big children — the pictorial version of Jesus' life, Jesus who is in Himself our mission.

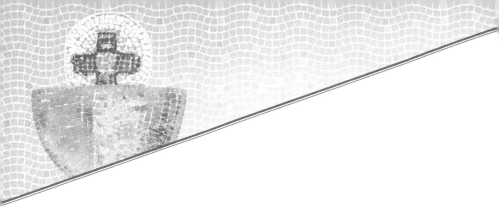

A Vocation for God among People[27]

WE'RE NOT LOOKING FOR the apostolate. It's looking for us. By loving us first, God makes us brothers and sisters and apostles. How can we share bread, a roof, and our hearts with our neighbor without overflowing with God's love for him? Everything is miserable without God. We don't tolerate any misery for the one we love.

What could belonging to God, who sent His Son for the world's salvation, mean, if not being an apostle?

However, we don't think about being apostles. We think about being the Christ we want to become in God's hands, in the Body of Christ, under the influence of His Spirit. This is the Christ who was never love without being light. He isn't light without the cost of that light.

We copy Him poorly, but we copy Him nonetheless. We are unlike Him but persist in entering into Him. How would we not at least be willing to be apostles and completely available to be missionaries?

We don't think that anything more is asked of us. But the same things are required of us more and more all the time, just as we're

---

27   A personal note, 1956.

continuously required to take away things that aren't Christ and what aren't of Christ.

Through a marvelous coincidence, we find ourselves made without being self-made, fashioned by love into something that those who are the most lost and blind can understand. We speak of this love even though we're not examples of it. We continue to be mediocre and unsuccessful simply because our actions aren't what they should be. They don't reflect Christ's splendor. We point to the person who is love. We cry out to Him that we love Him. We can shout it where every name has its place, but where He isn't named.

Will God continue to be "dead" for all those who surround us, those who know that we've given Him our lives, that we say it and don't regret it? Won't there be a "doubt" about this death?

We must remain people who delight in our own smallness — who laugh at ourselves when we think we are tremendous or act as if we are. There are people who place happiness where everything on earth seems to deny it, because their hands are full of God — or aspire to be — and cannot hold anything else. They can't be truly great, for none can hold a candle to the absolute greatness of God.

These are people who aren't hurt by the criticisms and rebukes of the Church because they are grateful. God wouldn't be their blessing without the Church, and they wouldn't be His blessing. This is because the Church is their Mother, and you don't blame the one who has given life for living poorly.

These are people who aren't restricted to any particular framework because love continually opens doors for them, lifts up their roofs, stops them or mobilizes them, calls them home or sends them on their way.

These are people whose homes have to be less than a tent, because a tent can be carried away. But they must continually be ready to leave their home behind. Their home must be ready for hospitality in the presence of the Lord, through the presence of two or three who are gathered in His name. It must also be ready for silence and for God's coming. It is a home that says: "I'm a home of the place we are passing through. Nothing more than that."

How could we refrain from evangelizing if the gospel is on our skin, in our hands, hearts, and heads? We're obliged to say why we're trying to be what we want to be and trying not to be what we don't want to be. We're obliged to preach since preaching is publicly saying something about Jesus Christ, our God and Lord, and we can't love Him and stay quiet.

How would we not work to make our presence felt in this light, fragile world? This is a presence that's ready for new beginnings, for putting down roots. If we know that only God calls, offers faith, and saves, then none of us has anything to sign off on. This occurs because we know that, ever since John the Baptist cried out "Behold, the Lamb of God," those who "follow the Lamb everywhere He goes" can be invited to follow Him to where they lose their homes, nets, and nations. It happens because as we follow Jesus Christ, He becomes the one who is our home, net, and nation.

We glorify God by calling Him God wherever we follow Him. But it's inevitable that we call everyone by his name in Him. It could be that nobody ever responds to this call. We could taste failure. But for the one who is God's laborer, all these tasks can seem to fail. And even still, the work that comprises these tasks never fails, for it is God's work. No failure is done for God.

But one of our tasks doesn't fail. It is the Cross. What was kept for us was "kept in Christ's Passion."

This is about loving — but not as an artist who doesn't make mistakes, who has no faults or weaknesses. You must "love God with all your strength." After exerting all our strength, we might find ourselves face down, defeated, and rebellious without understanding why. Redemption can't fail, but we probably won't know anything about its workings.

All of this is a life where nothing can assure us of living well, for nothing is weighed against our burdens. A hundred times, it will seem to us that we have held the earth in our arms, close to our hearts, and have passed through what other men call youth, maturity, old age, next to a blade of grass that hasn't even grown.

But eternal life will open up wide for us, and when we have to die — before seeing God — it could be that we'll see ourselves as small as a blade of grass.

We then won't be certain of our justice, but rather of God's mercy.

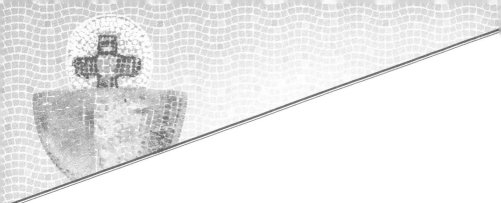

An Exodus and a Desert[28]

FROM THE GOSPEL'S PERSPECTIVE, the "world" seems to be in opposition to the Kingdom of God.

Going into the world and accepting the Christian commitment in the world is knowing, spending time with, and taking on all that's alien or opposed to God in each person in our immediate vicinity.

It's entering into someplace where, in a way, God doesn't exist. It's walking toward the unknown plan of redemption. It's walking as a person in the midst of people, but as a person who is inhabited by God.

This means that in his everyday life, the Christian is going to be in practical, daily relationships not only with living Communists, but with the force of Communism that resides in the minds and wills of members of the party.

The Christian will be in contact with the absolute and public denial of God.

God is proclaimed to be nonexistent because He is absurd. A collective mimicry of the faith proclaims Him to be absolutely

---

[28] A personal note written about an interdenominational meeting on the presence of Christians in unbelieving environments, 1959.

absurd and beyond reasonable assertions even where the Christian believes in an adorable God.

Adoring God means *saying "God" to* God in a single act. Everything that a Christian is made of and the entire way in which we're related to God are recognized in one act. In the face of Marxism, adoration is essential as a basic act of elementary justice. It's like being in the grip of a sort of "God-sickness," a kind of thirst for His glory.

Marxism's solemn denial of God invincibly attracts us in the midst of those who proclaim it. It irresistibly pushes us to stay among those who insist that God is dead, and to let the name of Jesus Christ, our Lord, who is also our living Savior, be carved in our flesh.

But the name of Jesus Christ, which is inscribed in us and written on our hearts, must, willingly or by force, become *our name*.

The name of the Son of Man and the Son of God is the sign of the extreme tension that we're going to undergo on the outside.

All that this name says about the *Son of Man* makes us welcome Communists more and more as brothers and sisters.

All that this name says about the *Son of God* makes us reject them — always as strangers and often as enemies.

The immense solitude of rejection which took hold of us is coupled with a solitude of love. "Because we do not belong to the world, the world hates us." It despises us as partly nonexistent, like something dead that can necrotize anything it touches.

We hope then that the Church will break this solitude that people impose on us, and that she will be mysteriously recognized. We hope our brothers and sisters in the faith will be a faithful presence for us even if they are not in contact with us.

But we forget that the Church is, by nature, alien to this world. The temporal realm, as voluminous as it is, is only an accidental part of her. As nomads and pilgrims, her human law is permanently marked as *temporary*. To the extent that she becomes a fellow citizen of people, of the world's pressure, and of the Spirit of God — and sometimes only the Spirit of God — the Church must cross new borders, face new exoduses, and pursue her Promised Land. These are promises Jesus Christ made to the ends of the earth.

She doesn't live this impractically. She needs our flesh, blood, and hearts. She continually needs some of her children to experience it.

Those of her children that the Spirit steers and sends move away from all that signifies the City of God in her and all that heralds the homeland of eternity.

Their brothers and sisters no longer easily perceive them and hardly recognize them. Who can take a bud or a vine to be his brother or sister?

They only recognize their unity through faith.

We become solitary through the very life we receive from a community that's more and more present but increasingly buried in the mystery of faith.

This solitude is endured among people we love more and more in lands where there are no obstacles to this love. These people are our brothers and sisters. They sometimes suffer, are often blind, and are always beloved.

The cross explains and resolves the tension of every Christian commitment. It's our normal Christian equilibrium.

This is why we become aware of the cross of this exodus — this exodus in our own world.

It's planted where the public evil of Communism is integrated — between the two commandments of love that God insists are inseparable and distinct.

Communism asserts the second commandment while rejecting the first one.

Communism wants to buy what the love of God is for at the expense of hating God.

Communism wants to give people what it calls happiness. But the fundamental condition that it requires is the death of God.

This rejection of God and worship of man, this hatred of God and devotion to man, and this triumph of man and execution of God are offered, explained, and exalted in an orchestration of ideological propaganda. They are clarified by the crossfires of dazzling illuminations.

We must bear this propaganda and these illuminations that can move, disturb, and solicit human passions that wouldn't be useful in us. This can be something easy, or something very hard.

Communism doesn't leave the second commandment of love intact. We're tempted here as well.

Love overruns all our human measures because it is love.

The neighbor that Jesus endlessly shows us

✠ is everyone,
✠ is *always* for everyone,
✠ reaches everyone's real needs and
   goes as far as sharing our lives,
✠ lasts as long as our lives haven't
   been completely scattered.

Fraternal love is like a viaduct that connects God and His people in a single circuit. We cannot divide this circuit without cutting it off from its divine source. It is one.

This is why Marxist solidarity doesn't respond to manifestations of brotherly love.

Neither every man nor all men have the right to life in Marxist ideology. What has the right to live, what provides the conviction necessary for working toward universal happiness, is the future, understood in a historical and immanent sense.

In order for this conviction to remain pure and active, everything that doesn't conform to it must be sacrificed — namely, a little bit of each person and a part of all humanity.

The same propaganda assails every Christian. It is aimed at each word where Jesus Christ expresses, illustrates, solidifies, and illuminates His law in the Christian. This isn't without risk or pain.

But both commandments of love increasingly become the indisputable manifestation of God's will for us.

To obey and be subject to their requirements clearly becomes what is offered to us and our brothers and sisters to glorify God.

That's when we realize the need for faith.

In order to experience God's love, we *only* need faith, but we must have *the whole* faith.

The faith — this treasure that we've received and that the world is lacking, which we must bring with us into the world.

The faith — because in order to sink into the world through our borders — into the world that is our neighbor — all maps are useless. Every new world is without it.

The faith — because everything God hasn't authenticated becomes heavy. It not only doesn't help us, but in fact impedes us.

The faith — because it is what it says that we must repeat — and nothing less — but with other words in another life.

A Mournful Song of the Saving Pines[29]

> Thanks to the roots of the pines, the province of
> Landes was protected from the sea. The first row
> of pines was burned and uprooted in front of the
> great dunes.

Enough, earth, we've suffered too much.
Let the wind come, and may it give back to the sea
These bones that are hung at the gibbet roots.
Our shaky bones with the skull hanging down
In this abyss where You mark the obscure and heavy
Steps of Your divine walks.

> There was a time when a call rang out.
> We were chosen in the living forests,
> And our bodies that were torn from the wind of the young plants
> Were welded to salt plains.

[29] Most of this symbolic poem was conceived and written as far back as 1927.
Almost thirty years later, Madeleine was preoccupied by the problems of a
Christian presence in an unbelieving environment. She had to resume this
ancient meditation and add the last two verses to it. It's remarkable that
very soon she sensed the religious uniqueness of some exceptional apostolic
callings. This intuition was probably from her own religious experience.

Enough, tides, enough, you drunken waves
That throw up the slime of your surges
On our clear resounding bed.
Enough of your arms and thick breasts
That the same caresses bang together!
Let the wind come, and may it return us to the sea.

It is to convey unbreakable messages
That we have, time and time again,
Before the voracious and rising waves,
Contorted the wood where our faces have lasted.

Riddled with rain and cruel storms,
Our pale, fragile, and mortal arms
Broke off like a lyre.
And when some hands pierced us with iron
They beat our flesh.
Our worn-out hearts smelled like wax.

Our brothers guarded the kingdom of the earth.
They were in unbroken blocks where splendor and silence
Let endless and dense life pass by.
Nothing tensed up, from their base to their neck.

The woods that were twined with oak trees and maple trees,
The gentle forest where fables hum,
Are protected by the shadow of their rows.
And in the peace of the safe enclosures,
The big apple trees that are made up of painted leaves
Stain the indifferent wheat with blue.

But when woods and forests rest from life
In this legal cowardice known as sleep,
When they get the strength and pride to turn green,
In dreams that are adorned with sunlight or frost,

Fruit salts and kneaded foam
Load our arms that have suddenly grown.
The night falls vigilantly and dreamlessly.
Our foreheads are stubborn — they are all the same —
Don't have any dreams that are haunted by false sunshine.
We focus on the shadow, and the shadow lifts us up.

We're redeemers of the sun, as it was intended,
Of the weak sand that the sea cherishes.
The sand that returns and mingles with the inexhaustible stream
And adopts it in endless nights.

We are upright, lifting our ravaged faces.
We are living on unchanged beaches.
Without remorse and doomed to the impure sand
Our love stops the debacle.
Our presence calls out the miracle
Of sand that's bound to its safe shore.

But the sun has very brutally excoriated us.
We've struggled and suffered too much.
Let the wind from the open ocean come and throw
Our mangled, sad, and grotesque bodies into the sea.

The soft sand dune that has been redeemed
Will share your safety.
Good forests and brotherly roots.
We, who redeemed you, have suffered too much.
We, who have been vanquished by the sand and sea,
Are returning to the eternal ocean waves.

August, 1927

On the ocean of days of cruel and clear play,
People arose with the suffering pines
They came to the same call and unpretentiously offered
    themselves
To save the wanderers who roll in the sea.

They held on for a long time.
Some bruised people slept in the arms of those who were
    willing to hold them.
They were crucified without a cross and suffered for a
    long time.
They really knew how to cry and keep quiet.
They didn't demand their father's house.
They believed in the only paths the desert creates.

But when the sands were established for their brothers,
On the redeemed shores of the eternal lands,
The redeemers, who were defeated, rolled into the sea.

June – July, 1955

Apostolic Action Today[30]

WHETHER WE'RE AWARE OF it or not, we're surrounded by indifferent people and nonbelievers.

People have stopped believing, have never believed, or are even unaware of what it is that they believe.

They are our neighbors.

Their very presence puts us in missionary situations — situations we haven't chosen, situations that surprise us.

Our Christian lives must become what they actually are: apostolic.

Not only are we not prepared for apostolic action, but we've been prepared for a life in which apostolic action seemed not to be needed.

Not only have we not been formed for apostolic action, but we've been given a formation that hasn't prepared us for it.

We know about "apostolic action," "the missions," and "apostolic occupations" that "proselytize," or the "apostolic activities" of an "apostolate."

---

[30] A note that was written for the intention of a French bishop, 1960.

We don't really know about apostolic action — the normal action of a Christian life near an unbelieving neighbor. We lived a Christian life, but we lived one among Christians.

We've been educated by this life. It's what we've been trained for.

Now, we have to transform ourselves on the basis of an obligation that we cannot refuse because it is part of the Christian vocation. This isn't done without delays, pains, or errors. There will definitely be errors in particular, because we are *practical idiots* of a supernatural reality — the mission for which God gave us the faith.

We don't encounter normal opportunities for apostolic action while living the Christian life *among Christians*. We don't generally experience it.

The mentality of our environment superimposes its evidence on the certainties of the faith. It seems that even without faith, we'd believe in God and Christian opinions through a fidelity to our families, our towns, and our countries.

That's why there's a muddled and mistaken understanding of supernatural realities.

- ✠ *muddled* — we don't make a clear distinction between the realities of the faith and the evidence of our minds.
- ✠ *mistaken* — because we know the realities of the faith differently whether or not they apply to our lives.

What the conditions of our lives don't remind us of escapes our attention.

Our abilities and strengths grow inconsistently. Those that are used and exercised become stronger. Those that aren't used or exercised grow weak and wither away. We then get used to a restricted visual field and allow ourselves to become inert.

However, real love doesn't sit still. If it's hemmed in, it increases the works that don't take place in this visual field, which has become a field of action. It thinks it's doing the right thing by accepting what's useful in place of what's necessary, what's optional in place of what's required, and proves itself to God at all costs. It's certainly right, despite the circumstances that deceive it.

This is how we restrict the supernatural life into a refined spiritual life. The inner life takes place inside us, and holiness turns into a perfection of ourselves. We do what we can, but only about what we know. This lets us remain faithful.

But if we change neighbors, or if our neighbor changes — if he's indifferent, unbelieving, or an atheist — we ourselves can't remain faithful without changing. We must *see* that he's our neighbor and *know* how to treat him as a neighbor.

Today, a restricted visual field doesn't allow us to love God with cleverness and a passive refinement without knowing what to do before a world that's abandoning God.

The faith isn't a luxury industry. It's a skill, a know-how for loving God by working for God in His work. We're charged with precise tasks in this work because God starts and finishes everything. He continually acts and doesn't give us the leisure to tinker.

But if our mistakes today come from a lack of knowledge, how will we know we're unaware? How will we know what we don't know if we're not taught what we wrongly believe?

Today we need, above all else, to be taught.

Later, and only later, we can wonder if the absurd dilemma that today's apostolate is having trouble with is a real or false dilemma. It actually seems that in the midst of contemporary apostasy and atheism, the Christian life can either react in order to survive, or act on the apostates and atheists at the risk of being destroyed.

We need to be taught, time and time again, about the Christian vocation and mission. We need to hear what the bishop would have to tell us in and for today's world if he confirmed us today.

If the Church were to exercise its very function of teaching in our regard, she would simultaneously teach us about the truths and realities of the faith. She would train us to experience their reality and educate us to act in accordance with it.

Then, we'd undoubtedly note that if our Christian life generally remains so incapable of entering into the world and overcoming its adverse forces, it's that it's not entirely and only the Christian life.

If our Christian life is often weakened, distorted, or destabilized when it works in the world, and if it abnormally wears itself out, it's that it's not entirely or only the Christian life.

In fact, in either case, this is about a Christian life in which some realities of the faith have been lost from sight, and sometimes they are the same ones.

In either case, it also involves anarchy in the values we place on temporary obligations and occasional means; most often, these values contradict each other.

Mission or Abdication[31]

WE MUST EVANGELIZE IN order to live in an atheistic environment.

Living in atheistic environments imposes a choice on us — Christian mission or abdication.

We didn't know there was a Gospel.

Christian environments are environments that have been evangelized. For a long time, they didn't need to be evangelized again. There wasn't any place left for the one who wanted to evangelize. The Christian who wanted to evangelize had to specialize, leave what he was used to, and go elsewhere. He didn't evangelize on the premises because it wasn't needed.

Nevertheless, he didn't resign, but his unnecessary evangelization remained outside his daily visual field. It froze the same supernatural realities on which evangelization is based in the same apparent uselessness.

In turn, these realities were lost from view because nothing more was expected from them.

---

[31] A conference note to an A.C.O. group, 1961.

In contrast, atheistic environments are to be evangelized. The more contemporary they are, the more complete the evangelization has to be and the more urgent of a priority it is.

Because the evangelization must be complete, it brings into view, in a practical way, spiritual truths that haven't been utilized. These truths become real and necessary for us again.

For the first time, these realities are about us. They remind us to believe again and to increase our faith.

They remind us of our Christian vocation and of our own faithfulness to God.

Evangelization is no longer out of the picture in this reestablished vocation. We're no longer to take it or leave it. Evangelizing becomes a sort of organic necessity — a priority and an obligation of our condition.

The Consequences of a Choice

If we consider this duty as a duty, we don't always know what it requires of us, since even yesterday we were unaware of it. We'll learn again what it is for us. Since evangelization didn't exist in Christian environments, it was ignored but not distorted. We can rediscover its bases and methods in all of their authenticity and simplicity.

We'll then at once distinguish between what we call "proselytizing" and all these apostolates that seemed like optional experiences of perfection — some kind of virtuous supplements of the Christian life. They were so distinct from it that they seemed to be able to be separated from it.

On the contrary, evangelization is presented to us as our body's natural reaction to non-evangelization. It's like the use of a living function and the adaptation of a task that fundamentally suits us.

Evangelization isn't a diversion. It's the fruit of a life — the normal effect of a normal life. We need all that we are in order to evangelize — just as the whole tree is needed in order to make the single flower.

The task of evangelization is the specific Christian task in an atheistic environment. Thus, the situation of this environment must contain the practical conditions of this task. They are the normal conditions and thereby become more favorable conditions for us.

Favorable Conditions to Reestablish the Authenticity of the Faith

Christian effectiveness honors God.

In an atheistic environment, everything seems to have been prepared for this effectiveness to be placed into circumstances that are exceptionally and visibly favorable. However, the interpretation of these conditions seems only to depend on a certain situation — the situation of the one who evangelizes.

If faith in itself doesn't change, progress, or evolve, and if we're unfit to improve or perfect the eternal life it provides us, the faith that makes possible eternal life makes people capable of it. They are all still people.

Faith in Jesus Christ is necessarily faith that someone receives and experiences. It's received and experienced in each "here" of the earth and in each "now" of time.

Faith that's experienced and has been turned into Christian lives must inevitably be singular and never identical. That which makes it invariable and unshakable keeps it diverse and moving at the same time.

If evangelizing reveals favorable conditions of the Christian life to us — even where we've seen disintegrating conditions — it's that it requires that we have a new perspective in which supernatural life is reestablished in the real laws of its perspective.

At the same time, we discover our neighbor's atheism and, because he's near, evangelization is required for us to love him.

We make this dual discovery again — without any preconceptions. We're not used to this dramatic situation, nor are we blasé about the call it makes upon us. Faith then teaches us about facts and through these facts — according to them and according to us — its eternal perspective, perfection, and relativity.

But the laws that teach us the faith in an atheistic environment aren't occasional laws. What they signal to us here as absolute, certain, and necessary will be absolute, certain, and necessary everywhere. What they designate to us as a basic obligation will remain so elsewhere.

What's here today that's relative, changing, and circumstantial will remain relative, changing, and circumstantial elsewhere and tomorrow. For all that to *remain what it must be* will have to *have changed* elsewhere or tomorrow.

Favorable Conditions to Reestablish the Faith's Integrity

The atheistic mentality is a mentality without God. God has ceased being an object of aggression, scorn, or curiosity for it. It remains only as a bald lie.

An atheistic environment is only interested in God from the perspective of faith. In an atheistic environment, faith isn't a symptom of the divine that one must chase away in order to thwart God. It's a human phenomenon that has passed its world-historical expiration date. If it has to be eliminated, it's because it delays and disables people from realizing their effectiveness as human beings in the present. The enemy of contemporary atheism isn't God. It's the believer and the believer's faith in God. An atheistic environment is contradictory for us to the extent that we believe in God. It's a live question that's continually prodding us. Its undertakings, research, and achievements continuously foreground the question before us. They interrogate the believer because everything seems to be going in the opposite direction of where he's going. He's disconcerted and very quickly tells himself: "Of what use is faith? What does belief mean?"

We're troubled because we're affected — in the very center of our weakness — by a faith about which we don't exactly know what it is or what it isn't. We're questioned about a faith in God that we've hardly ever practiced because it seemed a bit superfluous to us.

We're troubled because atheism seems correct in its judgment about us. We're aware of being antagonistic toward atheism because we've become anachronistic. We're residues of a bygone past that need to be eliminated along with every other antiquated artifact. We have no future other than to become fossils and ruins. All of this troubles our conscience, but we're unaware of it. We think that it is the faith that is being attacked, rather than ourselves.

If a test of faith is undergone on the spot, this is the one. It's like a laboratory test that separates two muddled realities that are unknown to one another. But then if we are to recover our faith's integrity, its visual field must be reestablished. This is undoubtedly not impossible, but if the desire to evangelize has already taken hold of us, faith will prove itself to us for what it is as it's tested. It becomes completely active in us because it is continually reacting.

The dynamism of our faith brings about its own effectiveness in us and outside of us. We learn "on the job" what our faith is and what it's for.

I offer two examples to help you understand what I mean and to support it.

A Healthy Inner Life

In an atheistic environment, the inner life is continually brought back to realities that ask to be believed and not imagined. These are realities we have to adapt to without adding anything to them.

We're continually led to practice the most intimate aspects of the supernatural life. It's not a spiritual life that's cluttered up with intellectualism. It's to be organized in relation to the reality of God.

This life continues to be *internal* for us, but it stops being *introspective*.

Autopsies can help us learn medicine. They can't teach us how to live. We realize that experiencing the inner life, first and foremost, is like striving to experience one part of our body separately from the rest — e.g., concentrating on our breathing or circulation in isolation from other vital activities.

We discover that the inner life is only — but necessarily — the intimacy of a life, of the way we manage it and of its dynamism and effectiveness.

Because our neighbor's characteristics make it absolutely necessary for us to evangelize, there's no longer any question about suspecting the apostolate or seeing it as the parasite of an inner life that would be a goal in itself.

The "you shall love the Lord your God" and "you shall love your neighbor as yourself" trap us between two imperatives that can't be incompatible because they form the basic law of our lives. They corner us into an inevitable action — work that we vitally need to do.

They corner us into the act of evangelizing — in a job where nothing belongs to us, but where everything must be done by us in the work of evangelization.

As a result, it becomes clear to us that the inner life is the interior and substance of a life — not only of its activities and movement. It's also the substance of a life that's fully mature — a life that does its work effectively.

The demands of the faith are finally gathered together and gather us together. They no longer divide us.

The Realism of Faith

The "neophyte's zeal" is the direct fruit of his faith. The neophyte's faith is the one we have to proclaim and not lose sight of. Ultimately, this faith is the one that will lead and strengthen our way of living.

Through it — let the unbelievers prevent us from taking our eyes off them — we realize what Baptism did for us. The seed it placed in us grows without being stifled, attacked, or hidden by parasites that we mistake for seeds.

Since atheism is a complete lack of knowledge in many of these environments, we must also evangelize them completely.

We're helped by this very fact — by evangelization itself — not to lose sight of faith's basic realities. Through it, we think about the unshakable land we have to walk on. We're better able than before at not getting lost or going off course.

The laws of our physical lives don't change either according to where we are or what we're doing. We know this. We know that our lives are a reality and that this reality can only be governed by real laws.

No matter where we are or what we do, we're there and we do it because we are alive. In order to live, we have to eat, breathe, and sleep. It's necessary.

How do we breathe, sleep, and eat? That will change according to where we are and what we're doing. There are daily routines that are suited to certain climates and others to certain jobs. Local or professional obligations will arise. But these are obligations. They are no longer necessities.

When we arrive in an unbelieving environment, we're taught about things that are relative, variable, and optional. We're not sure enough about what really needs to be done.

In order to know how to live, eat, sleep, and breathe, most people don't start by studying biology or physiology. An autopsy only indirectly teaches people how to live.

The Christian formation we need is to learn how to live by living, act by acting, and work by working. At the same time, we learn that the body is more than clothing and that life is more than food. We learn how to believe, just as we learned how to live when we were children.

If to believe is to learn how to live, we may have learned it in Vendée, and we will not be disconcerted if we go to live in Billancourt or in the Bourse.[32]

We won't act like lunatics. We won't want to work in the sleeves of our jackets, persist in living without eating, or — like the madman in the story — paint on the ceiling while balancing ourselves.

Christians have oscillated or fallen apart in so many unbelieving environments after having practiced these highly spiritual balancing acts.

A Note from 1962

Faith is a reality. We are the ones that wrongly make it into an abstraction or different kinds of abstractions, and we're mistaken.

We make an art out of it — an abstract art of living, a philosophical theory, or a system of thought. We turn it into an idea. Faith is a practical science. It's about knowing how to live *here* from now on.

We're continually mistaken about it. There's no pure faith. Through faith, a person dedicates himself and his life in Christ to

---

[32] Vendée is a region of France that served as the center of Catholic counter-revolution during the Reign of Terror. Billancourt is a wealthy suburb of Paris. The Bourse, literally "the purse," is the French stock exchange, and is used colloquially as a metonym for the global financial market in a way similar to the use of "Wall Street" in American English. [Editor's note.]

everyone's salvation. Faith enables him to dedicate his life in the Church to the whole world's salvation.

Faith is in time and for time — the time when this person's life is taking place. We could say that faith is the love of God in time. It is God's love entering into the temporal dimension of our lives.

Faith will be vigorously experienced by us only if our activity enlightens and strengthens us in the things that are momentary, instantaneous, and immediate.

Faith is for love. The life that it transforms from within is, therefore, a life that manifests and carries out God's love and bears it as a tree bears its fruit. This love includes the two commandments, which are inseparable and indivisible.

Faith and Time[33]

Jesus said the "words of eternal life" to each one of us —
in our time and for our time — today for today.

CHRIST'S WORDS "DON'T PASS away," but they are personally addressed to us in a human condition that passes away.

Christ's call remains the same for Christians in the whole world and for all times. But each one is called out where he is on that very day — in his life and in his own skin.

The Lord's commandments are unchanging. They require people to have the same new heart. But this heart can only beat with our old heart — only in our personal history and only at the time of our passage into human history.

Faith isn't experienced outside of changing and mobile situations and events. Love that won't pass away shapes the world through acts that are just as temporary as it is and embraces its human development.

[33] A note written for her teams, 1962.

When facing Jesus Christ's call, *the* good and typical response doesn't exist. There's *a* good response for everyone every day.

Hence the necessary diversity and mobility of acts that are required by the same faithfulness to the gospel. We forget this act in good faith as if a whole portion of our way of acting was "heard" once and for all and as if some words of the Gospel had received as a translation of its demands a translation that suited a place or an era.

Here are two examples: "You shall love your neighbor" and "You shall love him with all your strength."

"You Shall Love Your Neighbor."

Of course, it continues to be understood that "neighbor" — today as always — turns my heart's attention to *every* living person on the earth. As always, it asks us to be true brothers and sisters who really and concretely love all those who are near us. But the very reality of this nearness has changed. The one who is near us is the one we know, whom we can reach. The one whose needs we know about is close. The one whose life has entered into a very real contact with ours is close.

Our neighbor's "dimensions" have undergone an amazing transformation between what they were for an eighteenth-century Christian and today's Christian. We often act as if our neighbor was the one who would have been ours before the farthest ends of the earth became closer to us, when great distances were shortened by the advent of trains and planes and steam ships.

This awareness has disrupted some points of reference I depended on to choose and act. Thus, all that coincided with the love of the former little next-door neighbor was to be done without talking about it. What went beyond this same neighbor required a call or sign in order for me to take care of him.

In contrast, if the Congolese, Algerians, and Poles are my full-fledged neighbors, I don't need signs to know that I *owe* them what I owe my brothers and sisters.

"With All Your Strength," with All That You Can.

There's the same sclerosis in the translation of words. Strength for me — and undoubtedly for others — meant physical, moral, intellectual, and supernatural strength. These were so many areas that became clear at one time or another — a struggle against the waste of strength. This ran the whole gamut of the service of God from the parable of the talents to the parable of the barren fig tree.

But the strength that suits the strength of a person living in France today appears in the list — what he can do today and couldn't do yesterday. It has to do with contemporary human *power*. The same facts that change our closeness to people living today have changed how we can act. The boundary between what's possible and impossible has moved, whereas it hasn't always been changed on our maps.

All "our strengths" — the strengths of our past and present — must serve the gospel's basic momentum and its own movement — i.e., the Christian vocation's *movement*.

"Come follow me ... As the Father has sent me, so I send you. Where I am, you may also be. Proclaim the gospel to all creation. The poor will be evangelized."

"Come" — in your heart's freedom. This is a unique step for every Christian from all times and in the whole world. It's a personal and free response to Jesus Christ's personal call. It's an inner step that's always the same.

But Jesus Christ, who lives in us, dwells among us. He lives especially in the one who is naked, starving, imprisoned, a stranger, and homeless.

He has lived as an indefinitely displaced person in the history of the world. The one who joins or follows Him becomes a displaced person with Him.

Also, the Church must be where He is. Moreover, the Church has been displaced in all of its history through the violence that's been continually inflicted on her by events here and there. The Church has always been "oriented" but continually "thrown off balance" from its path by the exodus of poor people and the world's outbursts.

The Church is inherently magnetized by the ends of the earth. Whereas some of them are getting closer, others are discovering themselves. The extension of knowledge doesn't push back creation's limits — only the limits we've created.

These new limits of the world, which are new in our global society and recently appeared in God's creation, are being used to spread *the Gospel of the non-creature*. They are denying creation and ignoring the Creator. The meaning of man is being turned upside down in this approach to the meaning of the world and in the world. The Church must irresistibly bear down on these ends of the world in its mission of adoration, redemption, and evangelization, whatever the cost.

"Proclaim the Gospel to All Creation."

Unknown realities from yesterday are discovered today in man, who is God's creature, and in humanity as God's creation. Our increased proximity and the multiplication of our relationships have revealed the prodigality of God the Creator toward His people. We're so varied and have so many different gifts. The Church needs to carry this huge variety of life in her, because without it, her body would be unfinished and the glorification she owes God would remain incomplete. The gospel wouldn't have the impact to which it has a right in the world, the glory that only "a huge crowd from all tribes, peoples, and languages" can offer it.

Hence, the need to revise nonstop what we think of our personal choices in our own lives.

We often act as if God only had violent relationships with our destinies — as if God only acted through the pressure of circumstances and the disruption of events.

We somewhat think that abandonment to God consists of letting ourselves be worked on by these events and circumstances without thinking that we must also work on them — that we must make them our menial tasks. This is part of Providence.

World news — however it reaches us, be it through the press, the radio, or our relationships — must not only be facts for us to know about. It must not be some kind of sign that we look at with interest and bare intelligence. When we're facing it, we need to be the way we are at a post office counter. We see the backs of envelopes, knowing that our names must be written on one or many of them. Each one may be a concern for us and a summons.

To be capable of doing what needs done — whether it is nearby or far away — to *become* capable of doing it (not to have an absolute duty, which is opposed to distance, opposed to effort) is to be personally concerned and summoned to act.

But today, when we have to deal with accelerated events and dire circumstances, we should be alert and quick to see what we must do and where we must go. Without this rapidity, the most realistic intentions risk being obsolete before we've acted. When we arrive on the scene of an event, another event is already taking place there without our knowing it.

This view of things must ensure that everyone has an impartial and objective estimation of himself. What am I capable of and what could I be capable of?

This results in the desire not to mess things up — not to lose or waste what God has provided us. Our spot belongs to us and nobody else in these unique and fleeting spots of time. If we're idle because we're unconscious or blind, there won't be time for us to be replaced. Things move too quickly today.

Not being ready to keep track of the times is a sort of theft in relation to God. It's the most harmful of sabotages in relation to the Church. All our miniscule and cruel agreements are needed in order for a quarter of humanity to continue dying of hunger. The "apostasy of the working class" is undoubtedly the result of innumerable little thefts and faults committed by Christians who have been too busy with what they were doing to discover what they should be.

This meaning of "business" in God's business is found in some evangelical parables and is sometimes unsettling.

These spotlights on a few specific points can profoundly modify certain practical convictions, as they have done for me.

The neighbor God gives us in our contemporary conditions is a full-fledged neighbor. He has all the rights over us that the Gospel gives our neighbor.

As soon as people have become these "close" neighbors of ours, we don't have to wait for an inner enlightenment or a "providential sign" to love them tangibly as brothers and sisters. We don't need to wait for anything in order to "love them with all our strength."

The only limits are real practical or moral responsibilities — to love them effectively and concretely not only with all that we *can* do, all we're capable of, but also with all that we *could* do. This means *all that we would be capable of* if we developed some of our capacities, or used more suitable and effective methods, or made use of the additional strength that's available to serve people today.

This isn't about destroying ourselves and throwing our ashes on the universe. But for each of us, situations, relationships, and affairs — most often news or events — place us *in touch* with areas of the world toward which Christ and His gospel and Church are moving.

May the gospel be experienced and therefore proclaimed where *poor people* are assembled as a people, as nations, and as continents. This must be urgent for us. It's a permanent *urgent situation*, and the Church couldn't turn away from it without being falsified.

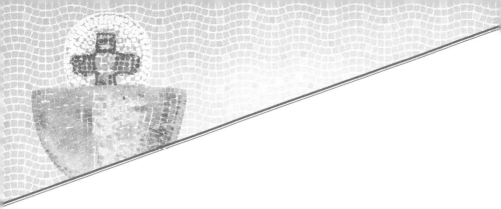

A Christianity That We've Misrepresented[34]

I'M NOT GOING TO give a presentation about Communism. I'm not going to talk about its philosophical, sociological, and economic aspects. These aspects are very interesting, but if I wanted to talk about them, I'd be incapable of it, as I don't know enough about them. Moreover, they are the subject of many studies. Books can teach us about these aspects of Communism or more simply inform us.

I'm going to talk about Communist people — not the "Communist person" or the "general idea" that we don't meet on the street, and not about all Communists; I'm not going to make you cross the Iron Curtain — but only about people who are Communists and live in France.

But speaking of Communists, I'll talk to you about people who were my immediate neighbors for thirty years.

So, I think I owe you more than a simply friendly report about the characteristics of Communist environments or the psychological

---

[34] Notes written in preparation for a conference for priests in Champrosay in June 1964. We're omitting some passages that are too simplified to be able to be published. They are indicated by a sequence of three ellipses.

or moral traits that are often found among Communists. Through this report, I want to pinpoint people as neighbors.

This is a neighbor who is as real as he is significant. He's to be loved and evangelized.

Along the way, I want to talk about how a Christian is to communicate with a Communist neighbor.

Perhaps some of these observations and reflections could be indirectly used for certain points of your research that my presentation wouldn't be relevant to.

So, we'll try to see:

✠ who the Communists are,
✠ why there are so many of them,
✠ the living conditions faith finds
    in a Communist environment,
✠ a possible conclusion.

Who Are the Communists?

We know that every one of these people is our neighbor. They are members of a universal body that exists, lives, and acts through them. Communism is implacably atheistic and fosters atheism.

They are our neighbors, whether close or distant. They include two-thirds of our contemporary neighbors. They are neighbors whom we're called to love as we love ourselves, whether it be the very day we meet them and whatever might be the gap that separates us from them. They are neighbors that must be present to our life of faith.

They are people we must get to know to the extent that we can. We must know who they are and what they have experienced, accomplished, and loved.

They are people in whom everything exists that God has always wanted for human beings — whether it's today or another time — even if it's mutilated or paralyzed.

They include people we've known before they were Communists, whom we saw become Communists, or that we've always known to be Communists. We may have known them to be indifferent or Christian. But they are people without whom Communism would not exist or act.

There's no such thing as pure Communism. It's not a philosophy that continues to exist, whether or not it has followers. Communism is inseparably linked to a conception of the world and a system of action to build the world.

So, the Communist supports this conception of the world. He's the agent that's inconsistently aware but always active in the Communist world. […]

Why Are There So Many Communists?

I've conscientiously worked on the questions that have been proposed in the program for your session:

- ✠ Communism is a *product* of our scientific, technical, and socialist world.
- ✠ Communism is a *response* to this scientific, technical, and socialist world.
- ✠ Communism is a *myth* of salvation.

The *product* of my work was something rather boring. These were supposed to be questions that were too hard for me. It was difficult for me to explain why I didn't agree with them. If you want, I think it would be better to take them up again in the discussions that will follow this report.

I think — and it may be a sociological heresy to say this — that Communism is the *product* of a Christianity that we've betrayed.

I also think — and it could also be a sociological heresy — that if Communism is a partial response to the sociological, technical, and social aspirations of our world, it's first of all a falsified response to the aspirations that God put in people's hearts and that Christ brought to light and life. [...]

We can claim that the main cause of Communism's mass appeals is that it differs from the contemporary world's characteristics and aspirations. It seems that we're the main cause.

Some nations, classes, races, and masses of people have seen Communism as a possible fulfillment of the human heart's hope — *the hope of the poor.*

Christ has given us the fulfillment of this hope. He hasn't separated it from the gospel of hope. He addressed this hope to announce His hope.

So, we've practically forgotten and scorned this hope. We've acted as if His hope cancelled it.

We've forgotten that poverty isn't a kind of inevitable privilege that's given to some people to assure them about the Kingdom of Heaven; that it's only a privilege when it makes people more free, and not when it destroys them by making them poor; that it's a privilege that's offered to us to share with poor people by sharing what we have with them.

We have not only forgotten that Christ wanted us to be poor before Him among the poor, but we have forgotten the poor as if they were distant brothers and sisters that we'll meet again in eternity.

We've forgotten that poverty in spirit — our poverty before God, the poverty that possesses the Kingdom of Heaven — is likely to be a myth if it's not accompanied by a spirit of sharing whatever the actions are that this spirit asks each one of us to do.

We've forgotten that without this spirit of sharing — a sharing of our lives and our material goods — we couldn't be witnesses to Christ, who was first sent to the poor. We couldn't announce the gospel of the poverty of heart.

The poor people's hearts were expecting this gospel. When the Communists raised their voices, the poor thought it was the good news.

The human heart is made for human brotherhood. Christ told us: "You are all brothers." He let us experience these words. He would not give us an ideology or a system of brotherhood.

We continued to be everyone's brothers and sisters. It's a fact we can't do anything about because God made us this way. But we've lived as false brothers and sisters or bad brothers and sisters.

Brotherly love is the visible reality of the Father's invisible love. It's inseparable from this love and is its sign and witness. People's hearts have hoped for and expected brotherhood where we've left brotherly love under the bushel basket. The Communists' "one for all" and "all for one" slogans were heard as the sign of brotherhood.

Communism emerged and developed in countries where most people were Christians, but where the conditions of life actually denied the gospel of Christ and where human relationships denied its law of brotherhood. Communism's apostles left these countries for an ideological conquest of the world.

The Condition of Life That Faith Finds in a Communist Environment

I've lived for thirty years — that is to say, half my life — in a Communist city. I was almost constantly in contact with Communists. These thirty years led me to make some observations about Christian life in this environment.

Not that long ago, I thought these observations were only valid in relation to Communists. Today, I think they can apply to most atheistic environments that exist in our time.

Christian life is *tested* in a Communist environment. They are reputed to be dangerous for the faith. The facts seem to prove it.

However, it would be absurd if faith couldn't be experienced where it hasn't been proclaimed.

It was not faith that didn't endure, but a life of faith that was modified, weakened, and heavy. It's a confusing life of faith that has been experienced for too long among Christians. Being a Christian has been reduced to little more than being an honest person.

Christians have been forced to experience the condition of the Church Militant in the Communist environment. It's the very condition of faith. It's the faith that makes us love the world to the point of offering our lives for it. It's a faith that's always alien to the world and an enemy to the world. It's often rejected by the world and baffles Christians. It seems to have transformed from the rock of safety to the desert of temptation. We don't recognize this faith nor were we prepared to experience it.

If what we call a trial in a Communist environment is what we used to call temptations, we find the opportunity for our own conversion in this trial. This is the trial of solitude, brotherly love, and faith. We learn God's *gift* to accept, ask, and receive. We learn that the gospel includes our etiquette and expertise. […]

A Possible Conclusion

Communism in 1964 asks us a question in an often boisterous and always explicit way. This compels us to respond.

> **Question:** "What good is faith, and what good are Christians?"
>
> **The Communist answer:** "Faith is a parasite and a lie. It makes people act against themselves by distorting their true humanity. It makes the believer in the midst of humanity not only a traitor to the human vocation, but also a bearer of bad, damaging, and contagious germs."

We need to respond to the question and answers that are posed and imposed by the way we live, speak, and act.

But the Communist isn't the only one to ask the question: "What good is faith?" This question is sometimes asked in *words* but always in *fact*, both in many the environments where we live and in contemporary atheistic environments. When a Christian or a priest — the latter even more, I imagine — runs into this silent question, he may not find a single person ready to hear his answer.

What is to be said when the question no longer exists, is excluded, and even no longer exists in people's consciences? When it's no longer being asked?

Yet this is what we must be prepared for. Perhaps the preparation could paradoxically involve asking ourselves one day, as if we're waking up from a dream: "What good is my faith?" If this has never happened to us — if circumstances have never put us in the situation of a catechumen saying yes at the time of his Baptism — I think we must do it ourselves in an urgent face-to-face confrontation with Christ.

Don't wait for too much or too little solitude to question you slyly or brutally. We must know that faith doesn't make us superhumans, geniuses, or heroes. It doesn't make us "better" than others — better organizers, builders, or thinkers. It doesn't free us from any human task, but gives us a job to do — a mission that's *for* the world, but not *of* the world.

It gives us the mission of putting the very love of God into the world — with "human ways" and "ways of being human," Christ's ways. It charges us with making God's eternal love real in the temporal world.

In addition to this, the "remainder" exists and must exist, but faith serves so that God loves the world through us as through his Son

He chose us to give us to the world that He loves, and we must love like Him, with Him, and through Him. This is what faith is for, which we're asked to accept.

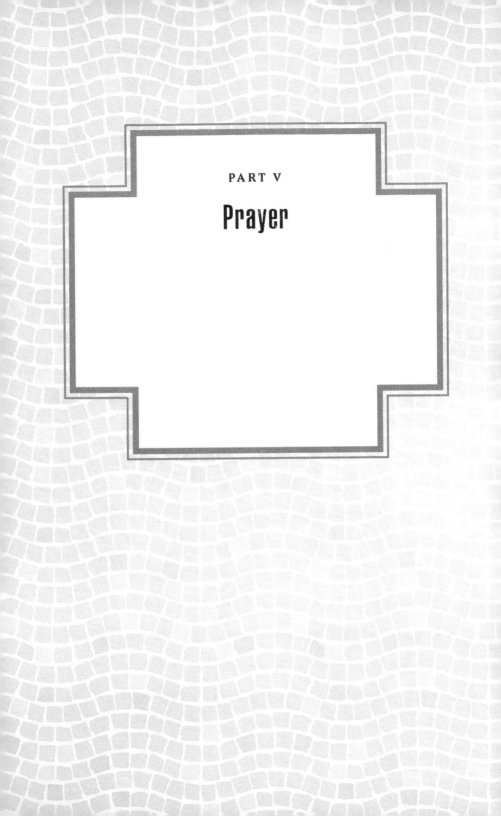

PART V

Prayer

The Christian expects from God what he works for with all his strength that his strength can't achieve. He asks God for His will to be done and His Kingdom to come. Prayer for him is the energy of his actions.

The Christian, an Unusual Person.

A Liturgy Without a Service[35]

YOU'VE LED US TONIGHT to this café called *The Moonlight* because You've felt like being here within us for a few hours.

You've felt like meeting — through our miserable looks, blind eyes, and unloving hearts — all these people who have come here to kill time.

Because Your eyes wake up in ours, and because Your heart opens up in our hearts, we feel that our weak love blossoms into a grand rose. It grows deeper, a huge and gentle refuge for all these people whose lives flutter around us.

So, the café is no longer a secular place — this corner of the earth that seemed to turn its back on You. We know we've become the hinge of flesh and grace that forces the café, despite itself, to turn on itself and orient itself toward the Father of all life in the middle of the night.

The sacrament of Your love is carried out in us. We connect ourselves to You with the whole strength of our murky faith. We connect ourselves to them with the strength of this heart that beats through You. We love You and them so that one thing can be done with all of us.

---

[35] A meditation written circa 1945 – 1950.

Draw everyone to us in You. Draw the elderly pianist who forgets where he is and plays only for the joy of playing well. Draw the violinist who despises us and sells each stroke of his bow. Draw the guitarist and the accordionist who play music without knowing us. Draw this sad man who tells us so-called happy stories. Draw the drunkard who goes downstairs while swaying on the second-floor stairs. Draw these slouched people who are isolated behind a table and who are only there so as not to be somewhere else. Draw them to us in order for them to encounter You in us — You who alone have the right to be merciful. Expand our hearts so that they can fit into them. Etch their names in our hearts so that they might be recorded there forever.

Later, You will lead us to the square all cluttered with fairground huts. It will be midnight or later. The only ones who will be left on the cobblestone will be the ones whose homes and workshops are on the street. May Your heart's leaps bury ours lower than the cobble-stones so that their sad footsteps may walk on our love and so that our love prevents them from sinking lower into the depths of evil.

All the illusionists will stay around the square — merchants of false fears, sports, acrobats, and monstrosities. They sell their false methods of eradicating real boredom, making all the gloomy faces look alike. Make us exult in Your truth and smile at them with a real smile of love.

Later, we'll get on the last subway. People will be sleeping there. They will bear a mystery of pain and sin that will be etched on them. On the benches of stations that are almost deserted, some weak and exhausted elderly workers will be waiting for the trains to stop so they can work on repairing the underground avenues.

Our hearts will still expand and grow heavier with the weight of these encounters. They will be heavier still with the weight of Your love. They will be molded by You and full of our brothers and sisters.

For the world doesn't always prevent our praying for it. If some have to leave it in order to find it and raise it toward Heaven, others must sink into it in order to haul themselves to the same Heaven with the world.

You set up a meeting for them in the depths of the world's sins. They are stuck to sin and experience a Heaven with You that draws and accommodates them.

While You continue to visit the gloomy earth in them, they climb to Heaven with You. They are making a strong assumption and are stuck in the mud, ablaze with Your Spirit, connected to everyone, and connected to You. They are charged with breathing the air of eternal life — like trees for buried roots.

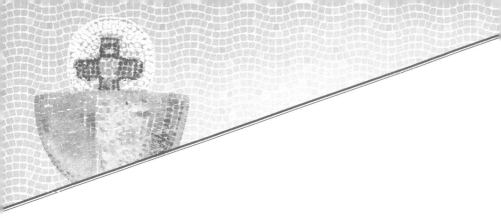

First Group of Notes on Prayer[36]

Prayer Is Our Belonging to God

MANY PEOPLE STILL BELIEVE in the logic and effectiveness of contemplative orders. Many also believe in a certain way of acting that serves as prayer.

But to declare that it's possible to live in a way in which our activities are prayer — as a continuation of a prayer which is only prayer, a time when we're "dedicated" to God, and snatched away from a thousand things that are reputed to be useful, in the midst of the world without being protected by a religious rule — seems to be generally utopian.

This would actually be a utopia if what makes a praying life didn't always have the same live fibers and if we didn't try to make them go through different circumstances rather than having them still go through the present circumstances.

It is inconceivable that an omnipotent God, who wants to be loved, would give His children a life in which they couldn't love Him. We're certainly the ones who are to be blamed. When we speak of

---

[36] Notes written for the intention of her teams, 1956.

"religion" and a relationship to God, we use our memories and not our ingenuity or our inventiveness. We behave more like archivists than realists.

Yet today we don't live the way people did a hundred years ago. This doesn't prevent what enlivens us from continuing to enliven us.

The same thing applies to our faith. It's given to people who don't live it out in the same way as before, but it keeps being the same life.

When there were no roads and even fewer cars, we could walk everywhere without the danger of being run over. It's been a long time since we've walked in the middle of the road. Yet dying by being run over hasn't become a scourge on society. This is because we walk elsewhere, and the danger of being run over hasn't been a sufficient reason for people not to walk anymore.

Today, it's true that we can't pray as we did in the past unless we're in a monastery or some exceptional life situation. However, this doesn't mean that we should no longer pray. It means that we should pray *in some other way*, and it's *these other ways* that we have to discover.

Prayer and the Human Being We Are

It would be enough to believe that God exists and believe in who He is. If He's God, then offering Him our lives would be disproportionate — not because we're giving too much but too little.

It doesn't seem that without prayer we can measure — whether or not we're Christian — the infinite difference that exists between the tiny living people we are and our Creator.

It doesn't seem that a healthy notion of the supernatural can be acquired without this basic assessment. If we haven't noticed it, there will always be some gratuitousness missing in our adoration. It's the sense of being an infinitely small and poor person who rejoices in grandeur and splendor. The only essential thought that he has about this doesn't let him rejoice for himself or boast.

If we don't have this foundation, our desire to become humble will lack a certain vigor. We won't understand that what we call "humiliations received by other people" are only specks of dust weighing on other specks of dust — whereas our life should cry out its surrender to God. This is the splendor of a God who is powerful enough to create something so tiny and who is clear-sighted enough not to lose something that's this small from sight.

Prayer and Faith

But we're baptized people. We've received the faith. For us, believing isn't accepting a "belief." Having faith and believing in Jesus Christ is to live the life of our God. God the Creator seemed to be shut off from us in a way — whether it was in His nearness or transcendence. Baptism made us His children. We were still just as handicapped but became part of His race.

This contrast is excessive for us. Our reason, while taking in the terms, cannot understand them. But faith plunges and sinks into this mystery. It knows *how* we're loved, whereas we only know *that* we are loved. This adherence to what the faith knows and our consent to what it tells us in a nutshell can only be understood in prayer.

Without prayer, we can't sincerely desire spiritual humility; we won't even know what it is.

In prayer, we'll perceive — if we resolutely ask God for it, and if we apply our heads to it — the considerable difference between what the most brilliant human mind can understand and what faith knows in its obscurity. Only prayer can help us thoroughly understand to what extent our mind is unaware in its greatest insights.

Prayer and the Church

The Church is made for who we are. We're people of flesh, spirit, and grace. Everything that's grace in her leads to mystery. Everything that's visible and tangible in her recommends that we undertake acts of faith.

Without prayer, the Church would risk remaining a social body for us and not the Mystical Body of Jesus Christ. We'd risk seeing it as a kind of army of spiritual battles where everyone has his rank, instead of a Body that we ourselves are members of, with its essential relationships, order, and values.

Without prayer, we wouldn't know to what extent obedience to living laws differs from discipline.

Without prayer, it would be hard for us to see that the Church is Jesus Christ. We wouldn't perceive what interactions we're invited to in her. The interactions going from others to us or from us to others are always Jesus Christ going to Jesus Christ or coming from Jesus Christ.

We wouldn't experience the Church without prayer. We wouldn't live from her as we're able to live from the speech after the Last Supper and the priestly prayer.

Without prayer, we couldn't distinguish the brotherly love for nonbelievers from this kind of inevitable love with which we most love each other as Christians. This is the unity of the Body.

Without prayer, the Church could give us all the treasures we've asked of her — the life of God in Baptism, the Blood of Christ in penance, all of Christ in Communion, and the blood-sealed unity of all Masses and their endless sacrifice. All of that would be given to us, but we'd only keep a portion of it without prayer.

Without prayer, we can be "scholars" of the Church's doctrine or some particular point of its doctrine. We could learn and retain them, but they wouldn't connect us with what should help us live better through them.

Prayer and the Gospel

Since the Gospel is a book, we have to read it. However, this isn't enough. The Gospel is a book we pray.

Our reason has its work to do in the Gospel. But our prayer has to receive the work God wants to do in us through it.

There is prayer between our reading of the Bible and our shabby attempts at obeying its examples and precepts. Without it, we'd see like nearsighted people and obey like paralyzed servants.

Above all, without prayer, the Gospel would be words, but we'd risk failing to meet the One we follow who is speaking to and leading us while we're alive.

The Prayer of a Secular Life

The prayer of a secular life is, unofficially, a public function.

So many environments are deprived of believers and adorers in particular. Even if we know that a Christian prayer is for everyone, those we touch and see weigh especially heavily on us when we pray.

Today, prayer is the greatest asset we can bring to the world.

Prayer and Our Love

It's all about love.

Love isn't possible without knowledge and does not increase without action. Every act of love has its own actions. The simplest ones require time. A mother doesn't put her baby to bed while peeling potatoes. A great love is almost always exclusive, because it can't be absent from the life of the one it loves, but also because it wants a little bit of this life to belong only to it.

Without prayer, we wouldn't love the God of love. We might be His servants, His fighters, and even His disciples, but we would be neither our Father's loving children nor Jesus Christ's friends and lovers.

Whatever the form of the prayer, it's through it that we meet the living God — the living Christ.

Whatever the human foundation from which it takes off, it must always use great obscure powers that reach God in Himself — faith, hope, and love.

Whatever prayer we start with — the Rosary, the Divine Office, re-flections on some book, or a particular action or meeting — as long as we orient ourselves toward God, the great supernatural forces are at our service. As soon as we orient ourselves toward God in truth, we need them.

Our reason in this field very quickly runs out of steam. We have to know that where our reason comes to an end, faith continues to move and knows. It's such a marvelous thing that we can pray and be very calm while knowing that our faith knows God as He deserves to be known — in our names and the names of many people.

When we become aware of bitter observations about ourselves, it doesn't matter much. If we don't want to languish in this bitterness, only hope can remove it from us. Only hope can prevent us from wanting our loved ones to experience the happiness that isn't bliss.

It doesn't matter what kind of prayer we pray — prayer as such, thinking, or action. We'll very quickly realize that we can't love God as we please if we lack His own love.

Faith, hope, and love are God's gifts. He gives them to whoever asks Him for them. Prayer that puts us in the presence of the living God — the living Christ — will be productive in itself. It will teach us why we love and urge us to ask for something to love.

Even more than the loving wife, every day and every hour, we want to offer this self-renewal — which is being developed by the one who loves — to be a continually rejuvenated new gift. To be seduced as we are by the one His enemies called the "Seducer," we'll have the passion to be like Him. We'll reproduce the smallest of His characteristics, thoughts, and actions in us. Where will we learn them if not in prayer? They are so often contrary to our hearts.

But How to Pray?

One day, the Lord advised His disciples to close their doors to pray. But another day, He taught them the Our Father on a road and among many people. He Himself prayed in solitude as well as in a crowd.

If a Christian knows he must pray in certain places — Jesus prayed in the Temple — he must also know he can pray anywhere.

The Sacrifice of Prayer

Prayer that's asked of us is a sacrifice. It's taking out time that is only to be offered to God.

This aspect of prayer is crucial for us. In our daily lives, it's the reminder and enactment of belonging to the God that we claim to have chosen.

Seen from this angle, praying is preferring God. It's also loving without deceiving others. For God wouldn't need our sacrifices — *the sacrifice we have to become when we pray* — if we didn't need to be redeemed. We're no longer innocent — we're redeemed. Our practical redemption still needs to be completed.

Finally, prayer strengthens our will to sacrifice, without which celibacy, obedience, and the courage to suffer would be impossible.

Solid convictions in this area are those that let us find a defined time each day for God alone. Real reasons for not finding this time can constantly occur. In this case other solutions — weekly ones, for example — must be found. If these reasons are episodic, we must then clearly recognize them and not let ourselves worry about them, but not dawdle when things get back to normal.

We always find the time we need to provide the necessities of life for those we love and for ourselves. We only find the time to pray, which generally seems possible for each one of us, if we consider it necessary. Therefore, we must first find out why it's necessary to find time to pray.

Prayer and the Relativity of Time

The most significant and striking conditions that circumstances of our era impose on prayer are a restriction of space and time. Many of our contemporaries have little room, and many have a lot of free time.

Having little room is one of the most unchangeable conditions of the poor in industrial areas.

As we desire to become poor, what must be astonishing is having room, not lacking it. It's praying broadly — not with specific personal intentions.

The work of people we call "workers" — although many that we don't use this term for work — has this particular trait. It not only invades their lives, as all contemporary work does. It cuts up this life for its own needs and leaves to chance the satisfaction of people's needs or the wishful thinking of the will. Having time for our lives is one of these needs. Being poor in many places means working at a job that doesn't respect the time that a human being needs for himself.

If we want to become poor, we must not be surprised by the major reduction of our time and, above all, by the arbitrary rules that govern it, or the conditions that are just as stifling for the freedom of our everyday lives.

Let's not deceive ourselves. Professional activities and wage labor devour our time. The professional can somewhat choose the way in which his time is spent. Wage earners aren't able to express their preferences. What we call free time ends up being wiped out.

From this, it's easy to deduce that the Christian doesn't justify taking time for God alone and must think he's unable to pray.

Resuming what we said earlier in other words — God didn't take the trouble to create us to allow us afterward to be asphyxiated in our relationship with Him.

Our time has air vents that belong to Him. It's up to us to discover and use them.

Anchors of Prayer

We need certain psychological conditions to see the weaknesses that enable us to contact God again. At the level of the contemporary modifications of our collective lives, we need to be aware of a transformation that has changed the very foundation of an entire part of our lives.

The examples that are taken from human relationships are well known because they are often cited. Other examples aren't as known, although they may be more instructive for us. They are to be taken from the field of certain primordial needs that people have — even if it's only heat.

We had to use wood for fires. A fragment of forest wouldn't have been enough. A space that was planted with wood was needed. Even when coal came on the scene, space kept its whole value. The length and number of mine tunnels shows this.

A new way of valuing appeared with other fuels that people no longer make through farming or the organization of vast spaces, but through plunging into record-breaking depths, through drilling and extraction.

When it comes to space, there's nothing less demanding than drilling. It can already have reached the layer of oil or natural gas and display only thin industrial rows in a panorama of pine trees and ponds. The drilling conjures up neither strength nor abundance. When people were unaware of gas and oil, they wouldn't recognize the value of the first spontaneous emissions. Consequently, they wouldn't put much effort into research or the development of resources.

I sometimes think that if the Lord were among us, He would use drilling for His parables. In the absence of this, we can imagine what they would be.

The gifts of God that we need to carry out His will are always the same. We're neither worse nor better than our fathers to be able to do without them.

Some of these gifts in our lives are always in the same place. For example, milk is always in cows and cows are always in fields. This implies that some space is needed — that of stables and meadows, in this instance. But other gifts of God that we also need can only be found in the depths in some places. In order for these depths to be reached, no more endurance is required than the work that's done in big spaces. But it does require as much. It doesn't require more perseverance, but as much. There are far fewer known risks, but an unknown number of unknown risks, which leads us to feel insecure.

In our lives, lacking adequate time and space, we must not look for the space that a Christian life required in the past. We're rationed what little prayer space that's available. What's lacking are the drillings that must replace it.

No matter where we are, God is also there. The space that's needed to connect with Him is the space of our love, which doesn't want to be separated from God. It wants to encounter God.

The one who hasn't tried to know *who* Jesus really, totally, and presently is won't want Him. He'll want Him less than a child in a grocery store wants an orange.

But there are those who have onerously ascended God's mystery and thought that it was possible, have believed it to be possible, and have ultimately considered it to be real. They have found complete joy in this mystery and have had to make more room in themselves for even more joy, while knowing that this mystery had become apparent to people's eyes in a man who was both man and God. These people know that this man dwells with them to the end of time with His Body, Blood, and glory. Those who have believed and do believe all this — we who believe it — would we lack the desire to find Him everywhere where it's said that we shall find Him? Would we not overturn and pierce all the obstacles that would prevent us from being always with Him more and more?

This desire results in prayer anywhere. Love bears the desire in it no matter where it is.

Loving God enough to want to be with Him and bearing this desire for love in oneself is having the strength that's capable of penetrating the hardest and densest life to connect with the one we love in prayer. A few minutes of this prayer gives us to God — and will give God to us for more than a few hours of prayer, which could have been quite recollected but weren't preceded by a vivid, intentional desire.

The retreat in a desert can be five subway stations at the end of a day where we've drilled a well toward these tiny moments. However, the desert itself can be without real retreat if we've waited until we were *there* to meet the Lord.

Our comings and goings — and not just the big ones, but the ones when we're going from one room to another, the moments when we have to wait, whether it's to pay at a cash register or wait for the phone to be available or for there to be room on a bus — are moments of prayer. These are prepared for us to the extent that we're ready for them. To have wasted them because we weren't ready must be called what it truly is: a minor sin. But if one day this is an issue about love and not sin for God, we'll perhaps become aware of having been odd lovers.

For these small respites of time exist for everyone. We women know very well what we use them for when we don't pursue the Lord. We dream. We have a solid reputation for that. Or else we're daydreaming — that is to say, we're thinking for ten minutes for no special reason about the Persil detergent sign on the subway platform. Or we dwell on our problems, or else we nurture our small setbacks. It's the time spent with any of these things that we need to recover and return to its rightful owner. It's preferring the Lord to a sign, a slogan, or oneself.

Living Doesn't Take Time

We'd need many comparisons in order to make it clear that time isn't the most important thing in the Gospel.

The time it takes people who love each other to say it has sometimes been very short. Each person may perhaps have had to go back to work or pursue some other obligation. This work or obligation only resounds with one thing: some words that are spoken in a few minutes.

If we've lost someone we love, and we find a letter or notes that teach us a little bit about his life, it seems to us that we've found a treasure, and our mind is really occupied with it as if it were a treasure.

If by any chance these notes are about what this person thought of us, thought for us, or wanted us to do, it would become our dominant preoccupation.

If, when we were little, we lost a father or older brother whom we knew through his writings, notes, and last wishes, meeting with one of his friends who talks to us about him and makes him come alive in his anecdotes and tells us what he did and how he did it would be a crucial event in our lives. This would preoccupy us for a long time.

The Gospel is a little bit all of that for us, or at least it ought to be.

If we want to study the Gospel from the perspective of history or higher criticism, it will take time. If we want to deepen our understanding of how the Church's doctrine is linked to certain Gospel passages, that will also take time.

But if we're looking for — which doesn't prevent us from looking for the rest — something about the living God in the Gospel that we don't yet know — more of His sayings, thoughts, ways of doing things, and what He wants of us, in short, more of Himself — it's not time that we'll need, or more precisely, it's *all* of our time, in a way, that we'll need.

Indeed, living does not *take* time — it *is* all the time that we live — and the Gospel, whatever it may be for us, must first and foremost *be* life. To do their work of life for us, the words of the Gospel that we've read and prayed over and that we may have studied must be borne in us for the time that's theirs so that their light may enlighten and invigorate us.

Prayer and the Sacraments

Sacraments that aren't preceded by and accompanied by prayer are like healthy food that's eaten in a confined home that we can't leave.

All sacraments actually change something in us through communicating what Jesus is Himself. If we don't look at the gift we've just received through prayer, we let Him make Himself useful, but we don't bring Him our desire to be regenerated. We're being wasteful.

On the contrary, because of this infinite something that all participation in the Lord bears in itself, the sacramental grace that's rarely received by force can continue to be a source of life and transformation that's proportionate to our hope.

The Mass and the Official Prayer of the Church

The Mass is Christ's sacrifice. Being a sacrifice makes it joyful and sorrowful. It's sorrowful because what Jesus suffered can't be taken lightly, and joyful because this sorrow is the reason for our peace as children of God, our reunion in the Father's family, and our access to love.

We already insisted enough above on the sacrificial character of our being available to God and how important it is for us to be willing to sacrifice. We've also concentrated on how impossible it is to separate this sacrifice from the love of the other children of God and all other people, so that the Mass easily reveals itself as our daily bread and the constant need of our lives.

However, in some circumstances and in certain apostolic conditions, the Mass can disappear, so to speak, from our lives, or rarely be present in them. Such a state of affairs can sometimes be accepted. However, it's very reckless for those who are undergoing this trial that they are not being helped by the actions — even if they are invisible but costly — of their Christian brothers and sisters or the support of a priest.

People are more or less attracted to the official prayer of the Church according to their religious temperament or personal grace. I don't think we can do without it without having looked into it.

In any case, not to be connected to her prayer and what has become Christ's prayer would be the sign of a weak attachment to the Church.

The liturgy can be splendidly evoked on the canvas of our lives in its yearly progression or the feasts of the saints. Even the "hours" of this liturgy can be easy reminders in the hours of our days.

Seven Minutes on Prayer

DURING A MEETING AT the Bossey Ecumenical Institute in Switzerland in July 1959, which included seventy participants, among them five Catholics, the representatives of different denominations had been invited to say what they most valued about the prayer of their church. Each one had seven minutes for that. They weren't to talk about either the Eucharist or the connections that prayer could have with dogma. Madeleine recounted: "When I was asked if I agreed to talk about prayer in this way, as I'd just arrived, I asked for time to think about it. I recognized my lack of knowledge of the "vocabulary" that was used by the people I was speaking to and the risk of misunderstandings. I added that I thought it seemed almost impossible to talk about prayer without talking about the Eucharist. This brief intervention marked the start of a very friendly relationship with the people around me."

We've rediscovered two sketches from Madeleine's communication that we're offering here. Comparing the documents will give us an idea of the rigor that Madeleine brought to express faithfully, with all due respect to her audience. what was dear to her heart.

I. What's Most Precious to Me in Prayer

I belong to Jesus Christ in the Roman Catholic Church. I'm in the Church like a limb on the body or a cell in a living organism. The Church transmits the life of God's children to me.

Living as a child of God in Christ:

✠ is being with Him and speaking with Him.
It's praying in a personal way.
✠ But it's always being in a family with the whole world at the same time. as we're in a family with God.
✠ For me, it's participating in the prayer of the Church.

This prayer is inseparable from the life of the Church, her sacramental life, the Eucharist, and the Lord's Last Supper, with which it forms a single unit.

The Church has *her* prayer. It still continues. The prayer of the Church is glorifying God and praying to God *because* He is God, a prayer that asks for nothing, and glorifies God in the name of the entire world while using God's very words.

The prayer of the Church is the contemplation and imitation of Jesus Christ, which is asked of me every day and every month of the year.

The prayer of the Church is the Word of God and the law of God, and the invitation to convert and obey Him.

The prayer of the Church is everyone's concern. It's universal. It excludes nobody. It's total. Nobody's needs are excluded.

The prayer of the Church is a prayer for me — a poor person. It keeps me from being fascinated by my egotism or particularistic interests.

The Church prays for everyone.

It permits me to silence my individual noise and be silent enough in myself to pray.

It lets me be constantly reminded of the real reason for Christian prayer constantly recurring — to glorify God *as* God and offer the whole world *to* God.

It reminds me of the supremacy of the love of God and of the next-door neighbor even on days when I want to or am capable of forgetting.

It gives me peace.

II. Prayer in the Church

It dedicates me to silence, which is the raw material of prayer.

It vows me to silence in its unceasing cries that are inevitably always unfinished and thrown out toward the Glory of God.

It makes me available to plead with my entire being for the needs of everyone I don't know because the Church intercedes and endlessly takes up the needs of all human beings — *each* need of *each* person *every* day.

It lets me be free of all baggage to pursue God. At the end of each day, I can leave everything I've heard, obeyed, misheard, or disobeyed from the Word of God. Tomorrow, the Church will give me this Word again, and I can give her a new heart to listen and obey.

It's in the Church that I'm in Jesus Christ and that I see Jesus Christ. It's in the Church that I live as a limb does on a body or a cell in living matter. My personal life as a Christian is a result of this communal life in the Church.

The communal prayer of the Church — the liturgical prayer — is inseparable from the sacraments. It's completely centered on the Eucharist — the mystery of the Lord's Last Supper.

As the Church exists for God, the prayer of the Church is prayer for God.

As the Church is in the midst of people, the prayer of the Church is prayer in the midst of people and for people.

It accomplishes the first commandment for God. It is the love of God. Love is selfless.

Above all, it's the greatest possible glorification of God, with words that are almost always God's words, on behalf of every person in the whole world.

For people, it's the sharing of the greatest thing we have — to be able to glorify God as much for them as for us.

This prayer is the contemplation of Jesus Christ — our obeying Him and conforming to Him.

This prayer is a teaching of the law of God. The Gospel is essential to it.

This prayer frees us from all egotism or all that distorts brotherly love — the love of some of our brothers and sisters — for it's always *universal* and *total*. It's for all of people's real needs.

Our greed, hardness, and blindness are all repaired in it.

For all people, as well as the person we are:

✠ It causes us to be silent in our hearts.
✠ It helps us be quiet within ourselves.
✠ It makes us capable of receiving the Word of God.
✠ It frees us of our habits and useless memories.
✠ It renews us in the face of what God wants of us every day.
✠ It lets us follow Jesus Christ and the mysterious call of the faith, of which she tells us *nothing* but the absolute and *all* of the absolute — even on days when we only have the strength to flee.

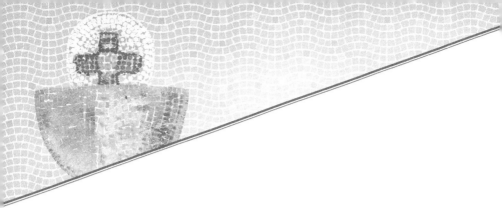

Prayer According to St. Rapture

St. Rapture was a woman from Bethlehem or Provence. We don't know if she was a virgin, widow, or martyr.

St. Rapture, who knew how delightful it was to find the Holy Infant, help us recognize God in the lives of people.

St. Rapture, who was delighted by such small events, such small people, and such a small child, help us to acknowledge the sacred history in daily events.

St. Rapture, who was delighted to enter into sacred history, let us make events which will be eternal with the moments of time.

St. Rapture, who was delighted to see God come into the world with people who, incidentally, came from other places on the same night, teach us that in order to see God come into the world, we have to see our neighbors coming toward us and becoming close.

St. Rapture, who was delighted to see God become the neighbor of your neighbor and yourself — one person among the others — teach us to look at this silently and raise our empty arms to Heaven.

St. Rapture, who doesn't bring gifts, but who offers everyone else's gifts, teach us to be useful without claiming to be effective.

St. Rapture, while you're being neck and neck with a tiny people where God has just been born, through your raised arms, give a real sense of purpose to the miller's flour, the fish seller's fish, the hunter's rabbits, the blind person's darkened eyes, the sinner's soiled heart, and even the police officer's police stations.

Help us to raise our arms with you to acclaim, as you do, God who made the world and comes into the world.

Christmas, 1961

Second Group of Notes on Prayer[37]

Praying Is a Gift from God

LORD, TEACH US TO *pray.*

There's no "certificate of professional competence" for prayer.

For internal or external reasons, we, at one time or another, have to agree that we don't know how to pray or can't do it.

We must:

✠ *Believe* that prayer is absolutely necessary in order for Christ's life to be vibrant, active, and fruitful in us. The certainty of this need is a consequence of our faith. Prayer is given to us like faith and with faith. If we don't *ask* for prayer, it remains at a stalemate. If we stop asking for it, it fades and "leaves our spirits."

✠ *Believe* that in order to pray, goodwill isn't enough if it doesn't result in asking the Lord to be able to pray: "Lord, teach us to pray."

---

37 This second group of notes on prayer was written in 1964. It's the conclusion of a year of thought and research that was done with her teams to overcome the difficulty of praying in a hectic modern world. These notes are as much the culmination of these discussions as they are elements of investigations for all those who find it difficult to spend much time in prayer.

✠ *Believe* that in order to pray, our efforts in creating a need to pray in us are ineffective in themselves. Reading and thinking about it, contemplating the life of the Lord and His prayer, researching what He says about it, and being attentive to His Word — all that is effective only if we ask with faith for more faith, in order for us to be sure that prayer is a matter of life and "slow death" for us, and that without prayer, Christ's life barely survives in us. It merely survives in us, so to speak.

✠ *Believe* that in order to integrate prayer into our Christian lives, as eating, drinking, and sleeping are integrated in them, our attempts are powerless in themselves.

Attempts at a resolution (I have decided to …);

Attempts at far off preparations (as of Lent, I …);

Attempts at the organization of our time (at sunset, I will …);

Attempts at organizing our activities.

All these attempts will only produce "results" that are often artificial and always fragile if they aren't accompanied by *our prayer to pray* and aren't based on our hope that asks for the light to know how to pray and the strength to be able to pray.

Believe that we wouldn't even have the desire to pray if this desire wasn't already a gift from God. As with all of God's gifts, it's made to return to Him in "gratitude."

That grace that makes us want to pray puts the strength to transform this desire into action and into a real prayer in us. Grace allows us to ask — in a real and sincere prayer — to know how to and be able to pray.

Thoroughly Praying

Let's ask the Lord for prayer through a real request by "giving it our all" — by putting all that we have into it even if it's very little. This includes all our little strength, our taste for it, and the time we have for it. It entails all that we put in a human request that's close to our hearts — even if we do it on a day when we're dragging along, when a migraine is wearing us out, or time is of the essence.

In order to ask for what we really want, we do all that we can really do. This is enough. Let's ask for prayer if this all is almost nothing.

Prayer isn't the definition of the old hymn: "Praying is happiness. It's a supreme joy." It's not simply saying one's prayers.

Praying is stopping other things we're doing. It's, first of all, stopping what we're doing in order to talk to God.

Praying isn't separating ourselves from others and abandoning what we have to do. But it's looking at God, in effect, and speaking to Him face to face. We do this without turning our heads away or our backs on Him in order to look for someone or something at the same time.

Praying is dealing with God as we'll deal with Him alone when we die. We don't forget others at that moment. We don't leave them by escaping or being indifferent. But it's time for us to offer our lives — our "death journey" — in the world and for Him.

Praying is proceeding to a sacrifice that everyone must offer. The *sacrifice* of prayer partly consists of leaving behind those we're leaving behind and abandoning those we're abandoning.

Our whole selves must undertake this "leaving all." Our body has to indicate that we're turning toward God. The way it's done depends on each person and each moment. We can kneel or walk if we're tied down to a desk to work. We can sit if we're going round and round with "things to do."

Our attention must turn away from the search for solutions that are in the works — from specific desires for this or that or from what we think would be useful to do. All the desires, worries, and hopes that are in us must stay in us, but have to be at a standstill so that we can blindly go to God without any expectations. We ask the Lord we know for unknown things, which He always gives. But we're unaware of what they are. We only know they are the best.

We must stop saying *I* or *me* and instead say *we*. We pray in Christ and with and through Him. A Christian's prayer is *the* prayer of Christ. No living or deceased person is excluded from Christ's prayer. It utters the most absolute *we* that there can be.

In faith, our prayer must coincide with this *us*. It makes it participate in Christ's prayer, which makes ours be active and effective on everyone — with an action and an effectiveness that's inaccessible to us alone.

In this abundance of hope, we may seem to lose our footing. It seems to us that to *hand ourselves over* to everyone in this way is handicapping and *betraying* our own people.

But here again, we must *believe* in the hidden economy of redemption. Like all our Christian actions, our prayer is love of God. But it must be authenticated by the love of the neighbor and the whole world.

Praying Christ's own prayer in this way and accepting the mystery it involves is to pray as powerfully as we can for our next-door neighbor, and for ourselves.

Distractions aren't always obstacles to our openness to pray. They are often outside us — like bumblebees, flies, and mosquitoes. They bother us as they would bother us in an important conversation. Systematically chasing them and worrying about them can end up hindering our prayer.

Prayer and Time

God Gives Everyone the Time to Pray.

John XXIII said: "We have to make time for time" — for prayer as for every other activity. Prayer is a raw material in all that we do.

But how do we make sure that prayer has *its* time? How do we evaluate the amount of this time? How do we find this amount?

There's no live prayer without making the time for it.

But it's not the *length* of time that guarantees prayer. It's the *value* of the time — what else we could do with it — and the value of the time varies. It's relative to each era, person, and period of life.

"Man Does Not Live by Bread Alone."

We can draw many similarities in the Lord's words between eating and praying:

Staying at the table for a long time without eating does not nourish us.

Eating more than you can digest makes you ill.

We can't eat on the run all that we can eat on a plate.

If we don't eat enough, we barely survive.

If we swallow our food whole, we don't assimilate it.

If we don't eat at all, we die.

God always gives us *our* opportunity to pray, but it doesn't always correspond to *our ideas* about praying.

We surely have time to pray, as God wants us to pray, but perhaps not the time to pray on our own terms.

When God has planned a sandwich for us, and we want today's special, along with hors d'oeuvres and a dessert, we don't eat the sandwich even if we have the time for it, while we're waiting in vain for a half hour to pass by when we could eat what's on our menu. Sometimes we don't find the renowned half hour, and we end our day without having prayed.

The prayer of faith — the one that nourishes our life of faith — is a *living* prayer. It's in a state that's fully alive.

If we eat while "picking at our food," "sleep with one eye open," and breathing "without air," then we're merely sustaining our lives and keeping them going. We're not renewing or reinvigorating them, or letting them develop. This is how it is with prayer that remains on the surface and keeps us distant from God.

No matter how long it is, one act of prayer coming from deep within us connects us with the living, speaking, and acting God. This act of prayer renews, reinvigorates, and amplifies all we do while having sown it within the hours of our day. This act of real prayer will influence our entire lives until the next moment when God will recommend or solicit from us that we pray to Him again.

For living in God's presence isn't only living in an atmosphere where God's thought is present or where the desire to act according to what He likes guides the way we act. It also has to do with keeping our ears open and being ready to connect with the Lord as quickly as grace suggests: "The Lord wants to see you" and "God is sending you to this person."

The Holy Spirit asks us to do this by changing both our hearts and our circumstances. We have to have an internal ear and an external ear to hear His invitations and get there.

The value of "prayer time" varies. The minutes are counted either in old units or new ones. Whether we need a little or a lot, prayer time has its full value:

✠ when I sacrifice to God myself and what belongs
   to me (not others and what belongs to them);
✠ when it's a sacrifice of the entire Church — and with the
   sacrifice of the whole Church. (Prayer is fulfilling a function of
   the Body of Christ under the impulse of the Holy Spirit);
✠ When it's a sacrifice for everyone (see above).

But everyone must discover this time.

Oil Drilling and Logging Operations

Our whole life is destined to blaze and warm up. Wherever love has been received, it inflames our lives.

But if God is the burning bush that burns without being consumed, we're quickly burned if we stop actively asking for, accepting, and receiving the faith with the life of the living God. We must maintain the faith in the same way that we maintain a fire.

There isn't a book of "tricks" or formulas for this. The conditions of people's lives indicate their personal opportunities — their potential circumstances and aptitudes.

Religious life, no matter what form it takes, is arranged in advance to make time for prayer and have a set time for it. If it's a contemplative life, everything converges toward a maximum amount of active prayer. To "maintain the fire," the amount of time is so substantial that we seem to be destined to knock down entire forests and replant them.

But people — Christian people — don't always know when, where, or how to pray.

There are actually methods of traditional personal prayer that many people can adopt without breaking their lives up, stretching them thin, or cramming them full. But at a time when living conditions are changing so quickly, everyone must find his own prayer methods.

We persist in "wanting to do the same thing." This leads to doing nothing at all because it's almost impossible for us.

The small windows of time creep into the busiest and most turbulent lives. If we see them — and we don't always — we think that by gathering them together, we could create a usable piece of time. When we say it's "impossible to pray," we must find these small windows of time and use them *as they are*.

In much of the world, wood is the only source of fuel available for most people. Elsewhere, they have wood as well as coal. But some areas have oil. The surface doesn't count if we're waiting for a layer of oil. There's no need to mine thousands of square kilometers or dig a network of underground tunnels. We drill wells whose openings have a tiny surface, but we go as deeply as we have to in order to reach the layer of oil.

In the lives of many urban people today, prayer is only possible by drilling. The intensity supplements the duration. These energetic and dark dives move toward God through their depth. They are concentrated acts of faith, hope, and love. Their perseverance is a broken line, but their successive in-depth jumps arrive when God wants them to — where they can get a hold of God.

This Time Can't Be Something Improvised

However, we must not forget that drilling *isn't improvised*. It's improvised even less than the cultivation of a forest or mine. Once the layer of oil is known, we look for the land that's the most suitable for crossing. We provide the technical installations and tools. We get the equipment whose strength is proportional to the supposed resistance.

In order to run our lives and develop wells of prayer, we must *look at* the small available spaces *ahead of time*, identify the most possible moments, and recognize the ones that can best replenish the hours when our faith, hope, and love seem to wear out.

We have to make a clear assessment that if we get up five minutes earlier to start the day with God — as dumb and numb as we are — it will seriously harm our health. We also need to assess whether making a person wait a few minutes will or will not really hurt charity, if this urgent intellectual work would really suffer from the five minutes we'd divert from it before we start, if the need to clean or do the laundry could suffer from waiting for a few moments to let us pray, or if it would suffer from waiting if someone arrived to have a word with us, or if the phone rang, and so on.

We also have to plan what form of recourse to God would best work for us in these lightning prayer times. We need to predict how we can best place ourselves as human beings and Christians before God. We have to foresee which of our overall attitudes lets us surrender ourselves completely while we're going toward God.

Killing two birds with one stone by lying down to pray in case we're tired is commonsensical. It could be useful to take a very short moment before we lie down to make our body kneel and speak to God with words in a human manner — the "fruit of the lips."

Some of the most common prayers have admirable introductions — the Angelus, the Veni Creator, and many others. We may not need any of them, so we leave them. But if we're slow to move, they can help us ask for the impulse we need. Even if we're worn out or ill, joining our hands, for example, is the sign that our prayer isn't "pure spirit."

In the same way, our rapid plunges toward God during the day can need an act in which our body participates. This signifies our spiritual uprooting from what we're doing and our preparation for what we're going to do — whether it's withdrawing from the work we're engaged in, leaving the room we're in, or stopping if we're tidying up. We can perform even a small act of love during this prayer break.

"The One Who Drinks Will Drink Again; The One Who Prays Will Pray Again."

I don't know if my personal experience is the experience of a general law. But for me, these lightning acts of prayer have awakened the taste for it. They have put me back in touch with the source — the layer of "living water." They have sharpened the need to draw from it more and more. They have clarified how I could increase them. They have proven to me that what they brought was vital and *necessary*.

How? I don't know. They have led me to discover the need and *possibility* of prolonged periods of prayer which not only didn't conflict with my life, but have also made it more viable, because they have nourished it with what it needed to be alive.

The Equivalences of Prayer

It has been said that "to work is to pray." It could also be said that "to suffer is to pray." But working and suffering aren't automatically praying. For working and suffering to be prayer, they need to put us in a "state of sacrifice."

Prayer and the Word of God

Our Radical Need for the Word of God

The official prayer of the Church is the whole Word of the Lord as it is repeated, proclaimed, and taught.

A primary condition of our entering into and dwelling in this spirit of prayer is hearing, listening to, and assimilating the Word of God so that it can act in us.

We can't be adorers of God "in spirit and in truth" without hearing and learning about what He says about Himself through His Son.

We can't encounter Jesus in order to know, love, and imitate Him without a tangible, continual, and persevering recourse to the Gospel. This recourse has to be an intimate part of our lives.

Each of these deep orientations and basic intentions lead to the Word of God — primarily, the Gospel, which is its fullness. But God spoke to us and still speaks to us in the Old Testament, and we can at least be attentive enough to listen to and accept what the Church repeats to us in these words all throughout the year.

Listening to the Lord for real and for good is a question of life and death for us.

The Word of God and Amateurism

Amateurism is our greatest risk in relation to the Word of God because we have a "good conscience" while keeping somewhat in touch with it.

The parable of the sower must be a continual warning in a life that has to be born and reborn from this Word, and must find its steadfastness and strength in it, and receive from it every day not only examples but a direct itinerary.

To be an "amateur" in relation to the Word of the Lord is, first of all, to *take* it and *leave* it — to leave it outside of our spirits, far enough away from us, "on the path" — so that the light we've glimpsed in it doesn't influence our days, attitudes, and actions. We take a little dip in the Gospel and let its living water evaporate on us or in our towel.

Being an "amateur" for the Word of the Lord is again to "take it and leave it" and "let it fall."

We must not confuse an inner inspiration — a taste that the Holy Spirit gives us on a certain "track" of the thoughts, feelings, and wishes of the Lord — with the "desires" that are awakened in us to pursue an intellectual research of texts. We also must not confuse them with an urge to justify a certain tendency of the moment with quotations that are randomly picked, or with the simple inclination of our laziness. We "hastily" read what's right in front of us or at hand, and we close our Bible or Gospel with the feeling of having accomplished a task.

Being an "amateur" is even to believe for a while. We plow into an example and a call of the Lord, and we give ourselves a right to forget it as if what's always asked of us is only done from time to time.

Being an "amateur" is, finally, and perhaps, above all, making the Word of the Lord a "conversation" about Him — even with Him — and not a "conversion" for which we're told everything the Lord says.

Some very human comparisons can help us grasp what we're amateurs in.

The Bible lets us read what the Lord tells us about who He is and what He thinks and wants.

We claim to love the Lord, and it's true that we love Him. But let's look at what lovers do when a particular separation forces them to write to each other. Let's look at how focused they are on what the day's mail holds for them. Let's look at them grasping their letters and carrying them like a treasure. Let's look at them miraculously finding the time to respond with long answers.

Let's look at lovers when they discover a way not only to write to each other but to talk to each other. If they are expecting a phone call, the worst racket can't prevent them from hearing it ring, and they run to the phone. If they are near each other on the busiest street, they don't lose a word of what one of them says to the other one. If it's cold, we can't sense it when we're seeing them. If it's hot, they seem to escape the general fatigue that others are experiencing because of the heat.

Let's look at them again around a large table, in an animated meeting, or working together. Everything seems to be transformed into a party for them because they can talk to each other.

The Gospel and the Scriptures tell us what's changeless in what the Lord wants of us: "Heaven and earth will pass away, but my words will never pass away." It tells us what's consistent in the way of doing what He wants.

Let's look at the work of the people who aren't working like "mercenaries." Let's look at the time they spend learning how to work and their concern to succeed at what they do — the lawyer to win a case, the scholar to complete an experiment, the businessman to earn money, and so forth. Let's look at their prudence, ingenuity, and attempts to be intelligent and use their willpower in order not to "fail" or "miss their opportunity."

The Gospel is *news* — good news. It's new every day.

Let's look at others and ourselves waiting for news and trying to know about it and pondering what we don't understand about it.

Let's look at how we wait for news from those we love when we're worried and how we wait for news about the evolution of an international conflict, the causes of a catastrophe, the issues about the Second Vatican Council that we're more taken with, or the results of a matter we care about.

When we've looked at the attitude of others or ourselves in this way with issues that concern human loving, acting, and knowing, we'll better see and appreciate our attitude toward the Word of the Lord.

I don't think we're too proud of ourselves, which, incidentally, isn't desirable.

The Word of the Lord, Our Dynamism, and Our Journey.

The Word of the Lord isn't a "dead letter" in us. It's spirit and life. Every conversion is dynamic, transforming, and active.

What the Lord has said won't pass away, and we already have eternal life and will have it forever. But the Lord talks to us in time. "He's with us daily until the end of the ages." We're to listen to and accept His Word, which does not pass away. They are "to be done in us" — under a sky and an earth that are passing away. We're to do this every day with Him until the end of the ages. This applies to each one of us until the end of our temporal and earthly lives.

What we need to hear from the Word of the Lord is our "present day." This includes the circumstances of our daily lives and our neighbors' needs, current events, and the demands of the gospel that always *call for the same responses from us*, but in a form that's *renewed every day*.

We can't discern what the Lord wants from us every day through the Word of God by ourselves. Our contribution is to listen now in today's world and time to what the Lord has always wanted for today — for those who are alive today and for our contemporary neighbors. Our contribution is also to pray in order to see and know what God wants.

Our seeing and knowing is the work of the Holy Spirit. The Holy Spirit renews the face of the earth in us and through us if we're open, available, and docile to Him.

He alone can let God's will be a light for our senses. May it be love in our hearts.

The Holy Spirit brought it about that the Word was made flesh and that the Word of God became one of us.

But for the will of the Father to be done on earth in Christ through the Holy Spirit, our lives must be completely offered to the Lord and dedicated to this invasion of divine life.

This full gift of ourselves would be a caricature if it caused us to exist between Heaven and the earth — outside of Heaven whose hour has not yet come and outside of the earth where we wouldn't set foot — and even away from the spatial paths where rockets are going ahead of people.

This full gift involves the complete activation of all our abilities, aptitudes, understanding, hearts, willpower and patience.

This full gift requires that we be people who are fully alive, fully subject to the Word of God, and fully flexible and mobile under His Spirit's impulse.

This gift puts us in a state that's the very state of the Church.

The Word of God and Our Conversion

Jesus doesn't talk just for the sake of talking in the Gospel. He speaks to show us something so that we can *know* what we must do and *do* what we say we'll do.

The first words of Jesus' teaching are: "Convert."

This conversion is the Lord's work, but it's not a magical rite.

The Word of the Lord is effective, but it requires from us a free assent to this effectiveness. We must have the desire and hope it asks for in our hearts. We must agree to its effectiveness and desire it. This conversion, whether it's personal or that of a team, requires the same conditions. The only difference is the methods used to achieve these conditions. Moreover, personal conversion and the conversion of a team are interdependent.

We must *hear* the Word of God. For that, we have to "listen." But we must not take it back. We have to give it time and not be absent. We must receive it and keep it.

This is true for one's personal life and just as true for the life of a team. In the life of a team, the communal reading of the Gospel involves gathering around the Lord and His Word. Most often, the aim is the continual review of our lives in relation to what Christ is asking of us. Occasionally, it involves looking in the Gospel for answers to questions that are asked straight away.

In both cases, it's a question of letting our lives or decisions be available to what the Lord says or asks for. He gives us an example. We need to let our impressions, judgments, and impulses be *on hold* before Christ's thought and will and to have the intentions of Jesus Christ in us.

If a real prayer of petition or a real desire that's inspired by hope doesn't precede the common starting point for this review within us or this common request for guidance, there will be neither clarification from the Lord nor a real and realistic response from Him.

"Let it be done to me according to your word."

A single word of the Lord that's fulfilled in us is worth more than hours of discussions — even if they are heart-warming.

Whether we review our lives from a faith perspective or after we've asked the Lord about something, we must then *lend an ear so that we may hear* before and afterward.

What prevents us from lending an ear?

First of all, all the reasons that were alluded to about personal prayer. But also:

We think we already know what God desires. We sift through the Gospel for what confirms our initial conviction.

Or, on the contrary, we rely on our memories of it. We don't look for anything new. But we do reference work to rediscover something we had found in the past.

This, of course, isn't useless. Every contact with the Gospel is graced. But if we compare our attentiveness, the seriousness of our research, and our desire to know to those we bring to find some information or help we need for human business, the comparison most often favors the human business.

We're very far from running the risk of allowing the Lord to distract us from our occupations and, above all, from our preoccupations.

The word that's heard *must be kept*. Its effectiveness in us depends on the way we keep it in ourselves — like a seed in the earth that we are for it.

When we've made a decision — a resolution — based on the Word of the Lord and are motivated by it — when we've resolved to search for what the Lord said and did — so that this sheds new light on our lives and rejuvenates us, we must *keep* the Word of the Lord and be careful not to leave it on the path before it has germinated its shoot of conversion in us.

Likewise, we must *stand guard* over this Word — not only to preserve it, but to defend it — to protect it from brambles and undergrowth that would make us "believe for a while" and not long enough for it to carry out our conversion.

If so many discussions about the Gospel continue to be meetings of people who "speak and don't act," the reason is in large part because of our lack of seriousness and volatile willpower. This is because the "serious business of our Father" and the fulfillment of His will in our lives that we want to experience for Him comes after other matters that concern Him less, or that concern us most of all.

PART VI

Alcide, or the Perfect Little Monk: A Simple Guide for Simple Christians

HOLINESS!
SAINTS ARE FAILURES IN YOUR NAME!

–Alcide.

Introduction to Alcide[38]

THE PAMPHLET WE'RE PUBLISHING here isn't a kind of diary where Alcide would have written his thoughts about each day's events.

This pamphlet isn't a guidebook to the spiritual life either. It's a reminder. On the occasion of an event, a circumstance, moral shock, or nervous breakdown, Alcide takes stock of the situation. He saw how he'd missed the mark and wrote it in a notebook so as not to forget it.

He would have called his notes mementos.

Alcide is one of those people of whom it was written: "They often get caught up in tragedy, but very seldom take themselves seriously." Hence, the irony and lack of seriousness with which Alcide went back over some events he may have experienced by seeing them in a tragic light.

[38] It's hard to date this text because it was done as circumstances dictated. As of 1942, Madeleine Delbrêl had started to note thoughts from her life on the occasion of the day's events. She had organized them for the sake of her team. The first three "books" formed a single whole unit at first. From around 1948 to 1950, they were borrowed and recopied, and soon circulated in many communities, whether they were religious or not. Other notations were gradually added to them. Delbrêl considered publishing them, but didn't follow up on this project. She had written some introductory essays from this perspective.

Here, it is natural to ask: "Who is Alcide?"

I have to be honest: Alcide has never existed. Alcide doesn't exist.

But Alcide was made out of a kind of person who does exist, a person who exists among other people and who experiences the things we all experience.

There's a small Christian world, as there are small worlds everywhere.

But this small Christian world doesn't live in one compartment of the world — not even in one sector in the Church. This small world is made up of rich people and poor people, people who are moderately intelligent and moderately narrow-minded, hearty people and tired people, resourceful people and clumsy oafs, people who run by themselves and people who are pushed to run.

There are grandfathers and young boys, old mothers and fiancés, new homes and deteriorated households in this small world.

There are fathers and bachelors, parish priests and bishops, stars and gypsies and maybe legislators, bankers, tax collectors, abbesses, young monks, nuns, and priests. There are even people from this small world who have become popes and others who have become saints.

Alcide very precisely represents those who don't try to become saints but would like to become saints in the small Christian world.

For they have their own way of doing it — not that they have chosen it. They didn't have the option to choose it. For them, the means to become saints are sorted in advance among the ways that all the "big people" of the world and Christians near them use. This sorting doesn't pay much, nor do we pay much for each of the resources it contains.

Take willpower, for example. It's incredible how much it enriches a person. It makes people live, as they say, beyond their means. The standard object for them is goodwill. If they have "peace to people of goodwill" in one ear, they still keep what every reasonable person says in the other ear: "Goodwill isn't enough," and also what indulgent people add: "Oh, it's not that he doesn't have goodwill!"

They see some people next to them walking quickly in life — like people who know life well and don't make the same mistake twice — people who suddenly know what to do, why to do it, and how to do it. But they go step by step even when they are in a hurry. They have to keep reassuring themselves that they are on the right path — as people do on a map, whether it's in the subway, or on buses and streets. Even though they are small people walking with small steps, they can still love God greatly. For God is great, and loving Him slightly is not loving Him at all.

Alcide is the simple Christian in each of us. He's the love in every one of us who is impatiently looking for God in everything and everyone, where faith finds God but where mundane life hides Him.

How Alcide Wanted to Become a Perfect Little Monk

To be a little monk that ...
(illegible words).
Epitaph of Blessed
Alcide who died in the odor of
sanctity.

THE CENTURIES HAVE BEEN bent on destroying everything that could indicate to us what spiritual family Blessed Alcide belonged to and in what community such a disconcerting life unfolded. What's more, we're even unaware how such a life was canonically defined.

This is how learned quarrels are revived from one era to another to give this or that form of life the glory of having nourished and formed the beatified saint. As a reminder, let's point out the titles of these incisive studies: *A Priest, A Master of the Lay Life*, or *The Religious Life of a Layman*.

One single fact has been almost certainly reported to us about Alcide's life. It led him to doubt all human greatness.

Here's the account as it was reported by his first companions:

"A certain Alcide, having come to join us, declared to the one who was teaching us that he wanted to know everything about the importance that God gives to our importance. Our holy instructor told him: 'Go, my son, to the field of the dead, and praise and compliment them for the days when they were alive.'

"Alcide did this, and then he returned.

"Our holy instructor said to him again: 'Go up, my son, to the field of the dead, and really admonish and shame them and show them contempt for their miserable state of death.'

"Alcide did this all over again and then returned.

"Then our holy instructor questioned him: 'When you complimented the dead, what did they say?'

" 'They said nothing,' Alcide replied. — 'And when you admonished them, our holy instructor persisted, what did the dead say?' — 'They said nothing,' Alcide repeated again.

"For the glory of our holy instructor, we must publish the fact that since that day Alcide was no longer the same. Those who knew Alcide saw the start of his holy career in this event — a career whose heroic path is traced by Blessed Alcide's notes."

The Beginner's Book

DISCERNMENT IN ACTION

The little monk does everything as if that's the only thing he had to do to go to Heaven.

Alcide on a day when he was in a hurry.

THE NOISE OF THE WORLD

The little monk sees God's call on the phone.

Alcide: 11:30 at night.

SOME SUPPORT

Carry, don't bear.

Alcide, one day when his brothers were as unbearable as he was.

HOLY LAZINESS

Find your rest in God.

Alcide, one day when he was sleepy.

ENTERTAINMENT

When you can't dance, make your spirit dance.

Alcide at the end of a long workday.

MORTIFICATION

Add more salt or sugar and don't reheat ... only when you're in charge of the kitchen.

Alcide, one day when he thought the soup was bad.

HEROISM

Get out of your bed with the music of the alarm clock.

Alcide, one morning at 6:30.

Do what's good for everyone rather than improving what would only benefit you.

Alcide, one day when he had the taste of the sublime.

JOY

Don't measure your joy by your body's well-being.

Alcide, on a day when he was having indigestion.

CRISES

Ignore them. They will ignore you.

Alcide, on a day when he was feeling blue.

CONFESSORS

Remember that remedies are made for illnesses and not illnesses for remedies! He who has ears to hear, let him hear!

Alcide, one day when he was searching for "peace of soul."

PRAYER

Remember that we pray to make ourselves good and not to prevent ourselves from being good.

Alcide, on a day when someone came looking for him in the church.

HAIR SHIRTS

Start weaving yours when your brothers' treatment of you feels like velvet.

Alcide, on a stormy day.

DUTY

Don't recognize it by the pleasure it gives you. You'd risk never recognizing it at all.

Alcide on a day when he had to mend.

OUR WEAKNESSES

Have soft edges. You won't bump into things as much.

After a collision in the community.

VOCABULARY

Don't call your neighbor touchy when you call yourself sensitive.

Alcide, one day when someone made him feel sad.

Book of the One Who Is Making Progress

HOLY POVERTY

Don't cling to anything — even poverty.

Alcide, one day when someone lit a fire in his room.

The little monk prefers drinking everything we offer him rather than choosing to refuse what he won't drink.

Alcide, one day when they gave him Muscat wine.

OBEDIENCE

Don't wait to agree with your boss before obeying him.

Alcide, one day when he thought he was right.

Obedience is a little bit about the body and a lot about the heart.

Alcide, one day when he ran to do what he was told to do while moaning about it.

HUMILITY

Prefer not to look at yourself rather than cry about your weaknesses.

Alcide, one day when he had a taste for examinations of conscience.

It's better to accept a mediocre compliment from a neighbor than to blame yourself for something you choose.

*One day when someone congratulated Alcide
for qualities he didn't appreciate.*

The little monk knows he's like all the other little monks.

Alcide, one day when he felt like writing his diary.

The little monk doesn't have any ideas about himself.

Alcide, one day when he was looking for his personality.

SILENCE

Don't try to be quiet, but listen.

Alcide, one day when he had interesting things to say.

Say only what doesn't silence God.

Alcide, one day when he needed to relax.

The little monk keeps quiet when he can in order to know how to speak when he must.

Alcide, one day when he had some rather silly stories to talk about.

Real silence never spoils love.

*Alcide, on a day when he responded to someone who
was annoying him with monosyllables.*

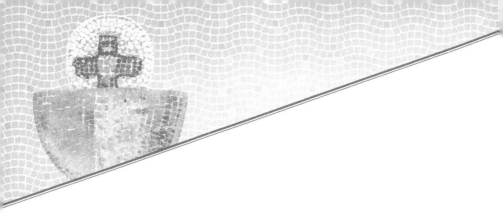

Book of the Perfect One

THE LOVE OF GOD

Loving God is being what God wants us to be and doing what God wants us to do.

> *Alcide, one day when his soul was romantic.*

God doesn't ask us to love Him in our own way, but in His.

> *Alcide one day when he felt like being a hero*
> *and didn't feel like being a brave man.*

When the little monk can't love God's holiness by being well-behaved, he tries to love His mercy even when he's being bad.

> *Alcide, one day when he'd done some foolish things.*

The little monk serves God in others with God in himself.

> *Alcide, one day when he wanted to turn his back on his brothers.*

The little monk isn't scared of anything because he's used to saving the whole world all the time.

> *Alcide, one day when he had to see a new gentleman.*

The little monk only does one thing while doing many things. But he does many things while always doing the same thing.

Alcide, one day when he wanted to go to the Sahara.

The little monk, when he is mischievous, rejoices in seeing nice little monks.

Alcide, one day when his neighbors' calmness exasperated him.

Don't be a hero. Be a zero.

Alcide, one day when he found himself to be mediocre.

The little monk doesn't ask God any questions. He spends all his time answering Him.

Alcide, one day when he didn't know what God thought about him.

The little monk doesn't persist in doing everything God wants, but wants all the world's little monks to do what God wants.

Alcide, one day when he was being zealous.

The little monk doesn't think he's capable of being a great saint or a great sinner. He thinks he's only capable of being a small part of the big Church.

Alcide, one day when he was meditating on his sins.

Because the little monk is hollow, he only knows how to receive.

Alcide, one day when he was looking for a vocation.

ALCIDE SHARES WHAT HE THINKS WITH OTHERS

The day of your profession isn't an arrival, but a departure.

Alcide, the day after his profession, when he felt like sitting down.

When you don't have a particular load to carry, you have to carry all the loads of the others.

Alcide, one day when he felt rather satisfied about his lack of responsibilities.

Don't look at your brothers to judge them, but look at them to pray for them.

Alcide, one day when his nerves were put to the test.

The novice is the tender stem. Don't forget that you're the branch.

One day when he would have willingly given up interest in the young.

Be even more what you want others to be.

One day when Alcide wanted his brothers' holiness.

You're always on duty.

One day when Alcide didn't have a lot of courage to put himself out.

Serving your brothers is reigning with God.

One day when Alcide wanted Heaven.

Be with your brothers as if you only had God to help you and as if your brothers only had you to help them.

One day when Alcide found that his turn to help often came back around quickly.

You're completely loving wherever you are.

One day when his humility suggested to him that his mediocrity wouldn't be very harmful.

Pray to God as if you were the only one praying to Him.

> *One day when everything was going wrong in the family.*

If we count on you for butter, don't forget that the food burns without butter.

> *One day when he had to eat the bread of shame.*

Know how to see the suffering around you, and ignore your own.

> *A day of crisis.*

Alcide, The Prior

"Hail, O Cross."

The first words of the beatified saint on the first day he was made prior.

JUSTICE

Beware of your judgment about those you don't appreciate.

One day when he was being put down.

If one of your sons doesn't trust you, don't be too quick to accuse him of a lack of judgment.

One day when there were boneheads in the house.

Prefer those who love you less. In this way, you'll have a chance to be fair.

One day when he felt as "dependent" as he was in charge.

Don't judge your sons' sins by the indignation they cause you, but by the pain they cause God.

One day when one of his sons had acted stupidly.

Walk in other people's shoes. Don't force them to go about in yours.

One day when he was dictating some ascetic rules.

The road will make your sons jealous if your heart is no longer with them.

One day when Alcide came home late and his brothers sulked.

If you don't have a good memory, don't forget to have a notebook.

One day when Alcide recalled an order he hadn't given.

The sickness that makes you ill doesn't make your brothers nurses.

HUMILITY

Brilliance doesn't necessarily clarify.

Alcide, on a day of eloquence.

Beware of ointments that make you shine.

*One day when Alcide found that his sons
didn't do things as well as he did.*

Know that it's a great joy for a monastery to have an incompetent prior if he relies on God while confessing his incompetence.

A disastrous day.

See to it that the monastery isn't given your name instead of the name of a saint.

One day when people talked about him in the neighborhood.

Prefer other people's criticisms to the solemn confession of your sins before your brothers.

One day when someone made an unfair remark about him.

God fills the center of the monastery. Don't go to the wrong place.

One day when he was pontificating.

Accept being a temptation for your brothers, which indicates you're a cross and a blessing for them.

One day when Alcide didn't please everyone.

If the righteous person sins seven times a day, don't be astonished if, being the prior that you are, you sin seven and half times.

A discouraging day.

If some people don't think you're holy, don't insist on showing them that they aren't any holier.

One day when very good people showed him that he was wrong.

PEACE

Your sons didn't come to the monastery to take care of your personal drama.

One day when he was fed up.

The tensions of your heart are reflected in the look on your face. Love. Then, your face will be ironed like a pretty, clean apron.

One day when he was told he had "a certain look" on his face.

You're not here yet. Don't force others to be here.

One day when he dreamed that everyone was rushing.

Let God act. Act later if there's still work to be done.

One day when Alcide had some ideas about his sons.

May every time you return to the monastery be a shower of peace.

One day when Alcide found many things done wrongly when he arrived.

AUTHORITY

If your son is acting like a fool, don't try to be an angel for fear of acting like a fool in turn.

One day when he was compensating rather imprudently.

Don't confuse God's will with your own.

One day when he had some ideas for reform.

Don't forget that weakness is the fear of harming yourself.

One day when a criticism seemed unnecessary.

Don't give orders. Ask for help.

One day when Alcide was too lazy to say: "Brother So-and-so, would you be kind enough to …"

Because you're in a good mood, don't treat your sons as if they were.

On a day of extreme friendliness toward afflicted people.

Don't forget to obey when you're commanding.

On a day when there was fantasy in the atmosphere.

Surrender to discipline, even when you're the only one that follows it.

One day when he was the only one at the table when the bell rang … and interrupted something very important.

Say things that need to be said, not things you like to say.

One day when he had many ideas.

Obeying your sons isn't obedience.

A day when he felt despondent and felt like resigning.

Beware of loving to teach. A father isn't a teacher.

A day of preachifying.

Prefer silence for your brothers over the gift of your words.

One day when he had many beautiful stories to tell.

GENTLENESS

The prior's anger doesn't bring about his son's justice.

Transcribed from Scripture by Blessed Alcide.

Don't make your nerves the home's bellwether.

A day when his nerves were playing a symphony.

Don't ask others to figure out the condition of your nerves.

A day when he was carelessly spoken to.

THE CROSS

When you cry for others, are you sure you're not crying for yourself?

An anxious day.

You're to console, not to be consoled.

A day when he was feeling melancholic.

If one of your sons is hurting, let him find you. If you're hurting, go find God.

One day when he would have preferred a dialogue to a monologue.

Beware of wasting time complaining.

A day when he found himself to be the unhappiest of men.

PRAYER

May your heart desire more for your sons so that God would give them more gifts.

One day when Alcide was a little disgusted with everything and everyone.

Don't do any spiritual direction, but direct your spirit toward your sons.

A day of pastoral activity.

EXAMPLE

A prior isn't a billboard, but a stone in the earth.

A day when he wanted to set an example.

You risk doing more harm by your sins than the good you achieve by your example.

A day of being ready.

FATHERHOOD

Don't waste time counting your sins when that time could be spent cultivating the virtues of others.

An anxious day.

Only harm one of your sons if it doesn't please you.

A day when a bar of soap filled his mouth.

Continue to be a father to those who don't treat you like a father.

One day when he wasn't being successful.

Don't say anything to one of your sons that could diminish his tenderness for one of his brothers.

One day when he wanted to unburden himself.

Don't strike a feverish cyst.

A passionate day.

Alcide, The Activist

LIFE TOGETHER

This is not for monasteries alone, but even for:

- ✠ families
- ✠ workshops
- ✠ offices
- ✠ parliaments
- ✠ rectories
- ✠ political parties
- ✠ trade unions
- ✠ Catholic Action movements

in short, all communities.

WAR AND PEACE

Learn the art of war on yourself and the art of peace on others.

A day of holy fighting.

Real enthusiasm is suspicious of bombarding.

When Alcide defended his movement.

If your voice is a bugle, your brother will hate the music.

During an animated conversation.

Just because you're a militant, your monastery isn't necessarily a battlefield.

When Alcide wanted things to run, work, and dance.

If you have adversaries, don't think they are armored vehicles.

After a needed retort.

The conquering air doesn't suit the holy militia.

A parliamentary day.

Strategy is one thing. God's ways are something else.

An evening of failure.

A militant doesn't have to think he's a soldier.

An energetic day.

OUR WEAKNESSES

Your brother may be brutal, but you're certainly weak.

While meditating on his moral bruises.

We'd be more patient if we felt more like it.

A day when blows came one after another.

It's all right to display hearts that are easily broken. They don't deserve holy struggles.

One day when his heart was being broken.

SILENCE

The first step on the mystical ladder of silence is to avoid hearing yourself talk.

During a brilliant story.

It's said that the next to last step on this same ladder is to listen to others.

The comment on these words has been deleted.

GREATNESS

Alcide was a man of his time — ours, that is. He was really enthused about the efforts of his contemporaries to promote all of the greatness of man. He tried to become great himself for the love, honor, and glory of humanity. From the start of his career, he was somewhat disconcerted by the gospel instructions. His rich personality seemed to him to be mysteriously taking risks. Then, he wrote these notes:

If you want to become small, don't despise the greatness of others.

One day when Alcide was annoyed by people's admiration for others.

If you find that you're little, don't conclude that you're a pearl.

After some unforgettable insights about his smallness.

Calling yourself extremely "small" is rarely being small. Truly small people know that they are in the early days of their smallness.

One day when, all told, he was being self-effacing.

If you can't admire your virtue, don't admire your remorse.

One day when Alcide hid away from everything to attend to his remorse.

The importance of great people doesn't change what you are. You're little because God is great.

One day when Alcide's heart was beating with admiration.

Don't arrive at the last place like the winner of the Tour de France.

On a day when he found himself to be astonishingly small.

Be little, but don't believe you're worth in grams what your brother is worth in kilos.

Look higher.

HYGIENE

It's important to discern the sluggishness of our spirits and our bodies' moods.

On a sad day.

If you lose face, continue. If you lose your head, stop.

On a day of contradiction.

If your heart goes to your head, you have too much of it.

When he was upset.

Three billion people carry the world's weight. It's useful to know you're not an exception.

Alcide was struggling against fatigue.

THE DUTY OF BEING AN ADULT

Becoming an adult doesn't prevent you from being a child of God.

Alcide meditating on the importance of his tasks.

If you tell your brother "I'm taking care of your packages," he'll be happy. If you tell him "I'm taking care of you," he'll be less happy.

A day devoted to education.

When you think of your brother as a child, you're being too much of an adult.

Alcide was stiff from looking at his neighbor.

ADVICE

"A counselor isn't the one who pays."

A proverb that was dear to Alcide's heart and was an introduction to most of his responses.

Letting your brother behave like an ass isn't respecting humanity.

A day when Alcide had been discreet.

ALCIDE, THE MISSIONARY

Don't forget that you've chosen what others have accepted.

When Alcide thought he was like the people from the Barbary States who surrounded him.

If you're only like your brother, you're not bringing him anything that's very new.

When Alcide made himself like others to bring God to them.

Money that's minted in your head rarely enriches your brother.

When Alcide gave to others what he dreamed of getting.

Think that you're right. Don't believe it.

When he was defending an obvious point of view.

If your outfit bothers your brothers, change it. But don't change Christ while changing your outfit.

One day when Alcide was studying the evangelization of a little-known civilization.

Tears are worth blood — but not all of them.

One day when Alcide was grossly misunderstood.

If you want martyrdom, while waiting for something better, accept this negative unforeseen event.

Alcide on a day when he was doing his taxes.

Masses don't have ears. If you want to preach, don't forget each person. They all have ears.

During a meeting.

When your heart is sick, don't remove it. When your stomach is sick, your fingers don't replace it.

On a day when he didn't think his bishop was understanding.

The Holy Spirit goes up and down. Don't block the elevator.

A day when he could have done without writing to his bishop.

If you want to make those you love be loved, love the one who doesn't love them.

When Alcide worked for peace.

God can want people to be separated. He never wants them to be divided.

When certain separations bothered Alcide's apostolic enthusiasm.

Don't say too many bad things about yourself.

On a day when some Christians didn't please him.

If your pocket is too small to contain the whole Gospel, take your bag.

One day when he regurgitated the rich for the love of the poor.

Give the heart of Jesus Christ to the poor. But don't forget to give the Blood of Jesus Christ to those who make them poor.

When Alcide strived to be merciful.

Others easily release you from your most difficult commitments. It's good to prepare to give thanks for it every day.

After his brief career's unjust end.

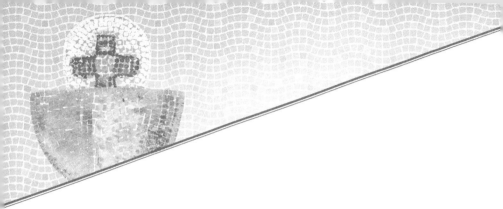

Life with God

RETREATS

When you're on a retreat, sleep is a necessary activity. However, it's necessary to have others.

When Alcide was getting ready to pray.

The Holy Spirit's light breeze doesn't necessarily smell like a mimosa.

When Alcide was contemplating a retreat in the sun.

God doesn't prefer to live in historical monuments.

Again when choosing a place for a retreat.

If you're good at comedy, beware of settings that are too beautiful.

More choices …

PRAYER

Distractions become prayers when we think about them with God. Struggling against them is sometimes more distracting.

During a time of overwork.

You don't miss anything to tell God what He wants. But you miss a lot to tell Him what you want.

Alcide was running out of time, space, and silence.

Talk to God instead of talking to yourself. You'll at least have that time to pray.

A day when Alcide was talking about feelings with himself.

If you think the Lord lives with you wherever you have space to live, you have room to pray.

On a day when the monastery was dangerously overcrowded.

If you go to the end of the world, you'll find God's traces. If you go into your heart of hearts, you'll find God Himself.

When He dreamed about finding God.

God has enough spirit. You can lack some. But He doesn't have any nervous disorders, and yours can be of use to Him.

On a day when his body's suffering darkened his spirit.

Praying isn't being intelligent. It's being there.

While listening to people talking on the street.

In order to find God, you must know He's everywhere, but you must also know that He's not alone.

Alcide willingly used this phrase when several things interested him or when several people annoyed him.

If you love the desert, don't forget that God prefers people.

While reciting the Rosary in the subway.

For those who are looking for God like Moses, a stairway can take the place of Mt. Sinai.

On each step of each floor.

My God, if you're everywhere, why am I so often elsewhere?

A short prayer to recite from time to time.

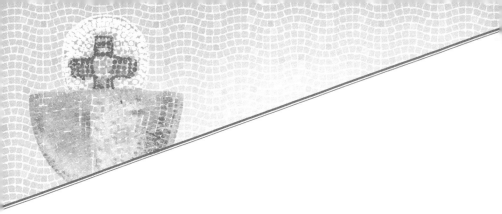

About the Author

MADELEINE DELBRÊL (1904–1964), Servant of God, was a French Catholic author, poet, and mystic whose works include *The Marxist City as Mission Territory* (1957), *The Contemporary Forms of Atheism* (1962), and the posthumous publication, *We, the Ordinary People of the Streets* (1966). She came to the Catholic Faith after a youth spent as an atheist. She has been cited by Cardinal Roger Etchegaray as an example for young people to follow in "the arduous battle of holiness."

Sophia Institute

Sophia Institute is a nonprofit institution that seeks to nurture the spiritual, moral, and cultural life of souls and to spread the Gospel of Christ in conformity with the authentic teachings of the Roman Catholic Church.

Sophia Institute Press fulfills this mission by offering translations, reprints, and new publications that afford readers a rich source of the enduring wisdom of mankind.

Sophia Institute also operates the popular online Catholic resource CatholicExchange.com. *Catholic Exchange* provides world news from a Catholic perspective as well as daily devotionals and articles that will help readers to grow in holiness and live a life consistent with the teachings of the Church.

In 2013, Sophia Institute launched Sophia Institute for Teachers to renew and rebuild Catholic culture through service to Catholic education. With the goal of nurturing the spiritual, moral, and cultural life of souls, and an abiding respect for the role and work of teachers, we strive to provide materials and programs that are at once enlightening to the mind and ennobling to the heart; faithful and complete, as well as useful and practical.

Sophia Institute gratefully recognizes the Solidarity Association for preserving and encouraging the growth of our apostolate over the course of many years. Without their generous and timely support, this book would not be in your hands.

www.SophiaInstitute.com
www.CatholicExchange.com
www.SophiaInstituteforTeachers.org

Sophia Institute Press˚ is a registered trademark of Sophia Institute.
Sophia Institute is a tax-exempt institution as defined by the
Internal Revenue Code, Section 501(c)(3). Tax I.D. 22-2548708.